...and **HE** made seven

In Our Circle of Prayer

...and HE made seven

In Our Circle of Prayer

Sharon Gooch
Darlene Banks
Mashan Minor
Tamala Lyons
Tiffani McDonald
Shontelle Banks-Gossette

Cushani Publishing, Inc.
Kansas City, Kansas

Published in association with Circle of Prayer Ministries.
Circle of Prayer Ministries
P.O. Box 901223
Kansas City, Missouri 64190-1223
816-420-9998
E-mail: circleofprayerministries@yahoo.com

Library of Congress Control Number: 2003111758

ISBN 0972849017

First printing

Printed in the United States of America

Cover and Illustrations by Lester Boyice

Cover design by Brion Dennis of Khemetic Design and Andri Jovan

Dedication

This book is dedicated in loving memory of our mother and grandmother, Melwee Minor, and our grandparents, Richard and Amanda Pollard.

We thank you for bringing us up in a holy environment, and for laying a spiritual foundation for our family through prayer. It is because of your prayers throughout the early years of our lives that we have come to this relationship with the Lord.

Acknowledgments

We thank all who encouraged and supported us in this project:

Our husbands, who regularly welcomed all of us into our homes.

Our pastors, Pastor Ervin Sims, Jr. and Mary K. Sims, and Pastors Frank and Robin King, who encouraged us with words, prayers, and as holy examples.

Lester Boyice, whose illustrations are incredible.

Beverly Scott, who was the first to encourage us publicly.

All of our family and friends and church family who kept asking, "Is the book ready yet?"

Our publisher and editor, Q. Elizabeth Gibson, who patiently walked us through the publishing process.

And most of all, to God be the glory for having chosen us to accomplish this mission.

Preface

The saying, "The family that prays together stays together," stepped from the realm of cliché to reality over three years ago, when six women (authors of this book) heeded the call of the Holy Spirit to unite in prayer on behalf of their family. They would fan the flame of the family altar that had been ignited by a praying mother and grandmother years before. Satan's attack on the family has proliferated, and the only way to restore peace and order to the family is the restoration of the family altar—both in the immediate family and in the extended family.

This book sends a powerful message to those families with loved ones facing health problems, financial difficulties, broken relationships, drug and alcohol addictions, teenage rebellion, and other family issues. No longer can families depend upon the once-a-week church visit to build a foundation that can withstand the onslaught of satanic forces prevalent in the world today. Far too long, many believers have relied upon the pastors, elders, and intercessors to defend them against enemy attack. It is time for family members to take up arms against the enemy, and prayer is a powerful weapon.

Humbling themselves under the mighty hand of God, the authors of this book have stepped into their prayer destiny—to that specific level of intercession to which God is holding them accountable. Wielding the mighty weapon of prayer, they have experienced miracle after miracle in their lives and in the lives of their family members. Their testimonies offer messages of hope and faith in God to accomplish the impossible. Through prayer, they are reclaiming their spiritual inheritance made possible through Jesus Christ, our Lord.

Praying in the Spirit, the authors go deep into the enemy's territory, whether at home or on the street corner in a drug-infested neighborhood, to serve notice on Satan that his presence is not welcome. They have not relied upon learned prayers, but prayers energized by the Holy Spirit, prayers that will penetrate the veil of darkness to overthrow the enemy.

This mother-daughter-sister-niece sextet has discovered the way out of wilderness circumstances through prayer. They each have bared their hearts to share with the reader the pain and agony of "doing it their own way," living life outside the will of God. But, thanks be to God, He has promised that when we seek Him with all of our heart, we will find Him. In Him there is deliverance from drug addiction; there is healing for the soul and body.

Through divine intervention, this family has set aside a special time of prayer in their homes to petition God on behalf of the members of their family. In prayer, they have experienced the awesome power and presence of Almighty God, as He meets each one at the point of her need.

I trust that this book will encourage you to form a family prayer group which will come together to lift up a prayer standard for the members of your family.

Q. Elizabeth Gilmore-Gibson
Intercessory Prayer Leader
Mt. Carmel Church of God in Christ
Kansas City, Kansas

Contents

Introduction

When we (six-member group) began celebrating Mother's Day and one another's birthdays, we had no idea that God was drawing us together for His purpose. We were just six women trying to encourage and support one another. Our group consisted of my sister, Darlene Banks, her daughter, Shontelle Banks; my two daughters, Tamala Lyons and Tiffani McDonald, and one of our brother's daughter, Mashan, and me (Sharon Gooch).

After a couple of years of meeting and celebrating together faithfully, our bond of love grew. We were fully contented doing just that when the Lord showed us the bigger picture. Through a vision, shown first to Shontelle, and then to Tiffani, God revealed to us the reason why He had brought us together. We were so excited and full of anticipation as we assembled to ponder just what God was going to do for us and through us. We were so amazed that He had chosen us. We were all serious about our own salvation, but had not considered banding together to present a united front to battle for the salvation and lives of our loved ones.

Shontelle's Vision

In the early part of 1999 I was living in a house next door to the house where my mother (Darlene) had lived as a child. The night I saw the vision, I was alone. My son was spending the night with his grandparents. It was late evening, dark and cold outside, but quiet. I was lying on the couch, reading my Bible about the story of Jesus' life and His crucifixion. I was so into what I was reading that it seemed as if I were there watching what was happening. I could see the crowd around Jesus and hear the roar of the people.

A couple of hours had passed before I realized how late the hour was. By this time I was tired, so I stopped reading and went to bed. That's when the vision came.

I could see six people in a circle holding hands. Four of them appeared as shadows, but I recognized each one. The fifth person was different, however. God allowed me to see her face clearly. She stood right across from me, as if she were the head of the circle. This person was my Aunt Sharon.

During the vision, the Lord gave me some specific instructions. He spoke to me about the many things that we needed to pray about, some of which were jealousy, envy, and the tendency to gossip. God also said that many blessings were coming into our lives, and that good things were going to happen to us, but He did not want jealousy and envy to separate us. God knew that the devil would try to come against us in various ways and try to tear us apart. He wanted the six of us to come together and pray for one another.

As the Lord was speaking, He let me know exactly who the six women in the circle were; they were holding hands, touching and agreeing in prayer. These are the six women God chose in the vision: Aunt Sharon, my mother (Darlene), my three cousins (Mashan,Tammy, and Tiffani), and I (Shontelle).

This was the seed that began our family prayer group. Thank You, Jesus.

Right after the vision, I invited my cousins over to watch a worship service video tape and to tell them about the vision. Everyone else found out about the vision around Mother's Day that year when we gathered for our annual Mother's Day luncheon.

Tiffani's Vision

In mid-October of 1999, the Lord woke me up early one Saturday morning with a vision, and this is what I saw:

> I saw the men in our family in shackles and chains, which signified bondage. Two of the faces I saw clearly—two of my uncles—but the rest of the faces I couldn't see. The Lord asked the question, "Why are there saved women in your family, and these men are in bondage?"
>
> I got out of bed and began writing as the Lord gave me revelation. Next, I saw the shackles falling off. The Lord said that once we started praying for the men in our family they would be set free.

After the vision, I was awake and began getting ready for work. En route to work, I couldn't wait to tell someone, even though it was about 7:00 A.M., so I called my sister. "Tammy, don't get upset because I woke you up," I said, "but I am excited about what God has shown me." I told my sister what the Lord had revealed to me and asked her to call the other four saved women in our circle of prayer and set up a time for us to pray that day. Everyone met at my cousin Mashan's house that evening to pray for our men. We chose her house first because she was having the most trouble with her son.

The house that Mashan lived in was important to us. This was the house where my mother and my Aunt Darlene had grown up with a praying, loving Mother. Their paternal grandparents, both also prayerful and very loving, had lived just two doors down the street. That night we planned where and when, and how often we would meet for prayer. Our family prayer would be one night a week, Tuesday, in this order: Mashan's house, first; Tammy's, second; Aunt Darlene's, third; Tiffani's, fourth; and my mother's, fifth (Sharon). At the time, Shontelle was living at home with her mom (Darlene).

We felt the urgency of God's message in our hearts, and we sensed the need to begin praying together. We came together in faith as an act of obedience, trying to verbalize our needs and seek His presence. God had told us twice to come together and pray, and we were afraid to procrastinate any longer.

As we prayed, God began to reveal many aspects of Himself to us on a personal level. We came to know Him as a healer, and our faith increased. We found Him to be a way-maker, and our faith increased. When we realized that our God was actually 'mindful' of us, our faith increased exponentially.

It was almost October of 2001 (?) and we were approaching the end of our third year of family prayer when we conceived the idea of writing a book to share what God has done for our family. This is how ...*and HE made seven* came about. The book contains the visions, testimonies, disappointments, and victories of six women whom God brought together through the visions of Shontelle Banks (Gossette), and Tiffani McDonald. Ultimately, this book was written by God through us, to be used by Him to bring salvation, healing and deliverance to families; and to build up God's kingdom and tear Satan's kingdom down. Through this book God seeks to encourage you and show you the importance of family prayer.

The six of us, brought up in the same family, answered the call of God on our lives to become intercessors. Having experienced many tragedies, each woman tells her story of the goodness of God and how He brought her through. Each of us had come to the table with her own experiences, personal needs, and offerings to the group, and we began praying for one another. As adult women, we carried baggage from our past: marriages gone wrong, relationships broken, hurts and wounds that have made each of us who we are today. In this book we share, not only the events of the past three years, but also some of our experiences of the past, some of the struggles and hardships we endured which eventually brought us to a closer walk with the Lord.

We all desired a closer relationship with the Lord, but we realized that we had to remove the clutter from our lives so that we could pray more effectively for one another. We repented and asked God's forgiveness for all our shortcomings. We began each session with scriptures to encourage us, listened to praise music to usher in the Holy Spirit, and then prayed. At the conclusion of each prayer, we would call our children, place them in the middle of our circle, anoint them, and pray for them. We always ended with a group hug and whisperings of "I love you, sister, cousin, auntie, niece, or daughter." We had always loved one another, but it was amazing to see how our love for one another blossomed as we met weekly.

Each week we would share prayer requests, and sometimes praise reports among the group. Not only did we pray for ourselves, but we also interceded for all the males in the family, from the oldest to the youngest. We prayed for their health, healing, protection, peace of mind, and, most of all, salvation. Our prayer was that they would be men of God and the heads of their households as God intended them to be. We prayed that generational curses, such as cancer, high blood pressure, alcoholism, drug abuse, and all manner of sickness and disease, would be broken off our lives so that future generations would be free of those curses.

Friends would give a member of the group prayer requests, and we would say a special prayer for their needs. Also, we prayed for our leaders, both spiritual and natural, and for many the welfare of the saints and world conditions.

When our group met for prayer, many times the Lord would have given us revelations as to how to pray and what to pray. Through the spirit of discernment, we could see one another's needs, and we would share a word of encouragement to the one or ones who needed encouragement. We counseled one another through rough times, prayed for one another through illnesses, and stood in the gap when a prayer partner was being attacked by the enemy. On prayer night, if one of us had recently moved into a new home or apartment, we would walk throughout the home or apartment, praying and anointing it with oil. We would rebuke any evil or unclean spirits and cast them out. Then we would ask God's Holy Spirit to fill the place.

Members of our prayer group learned the importance of praising and thanking God even before we would see the results of our prayer, just repeating His Word back to Him: "Again I say unto you, that if two of you shall agree on earth as touching anything that they shall ask, it shall be done for them of my Father which is in heaven" (Matt. 18:19).

As the weeks turned into months and the months into years, we increasingly learned how to seek the face of God, how to pray and what to pray. We learned to be specific in our prayers. We finally understood that it pleases God that we come to Him with prayer and supplication. In Hebrews 10:23, His words encourage us to "...hold fast the profession of our faith without wavering; (for he is faithful that promised)." When we look back over the past few years, we know that we have been truly blessed, not that we haven't been through some rough times, but that God has been faithful to bring us through them all.

Throughout the pages of this book, you will learn about each woman, one by one, as she shares victorious testimonies of an awesome God. We trust that you will be blessed as you share God's revelation of Himself to us. Our testimonies can be summed up in the following verses of Scripture:

That which we have seen and heard
declare we unto you, that ye also may have

fellowship with us: and truly our fellowship is with the Father, and with his Son Jesus Christ. And these things write we unto you, that your joy may be full (I John 1:3, 4).

How Our Book Received Its Title

One Thursday night after prayer, we were sitting around talking, reflecting on God's goodness. A question dropped into my spirit to ask the group: "What is the significance of the number six?" God had chosen six of us, the number could easily have been three or four.

My Aunt Darlene answered, "He just knew what it would take."

"No, the answer is deeper than that," I said. "Let's pray and ask God what it is."

My sister, Tammy, was sitting on the floor with her eyes closed, as if she were meditating. I asked her if she had understood what I was getting at, and she nodded her head yes. She shared that she had always felt that God made seven in our group, and that He was our completion—the six of us and the Lord. My sister's words just did something to my spirit. I got up, went over to my aunt, and said, "Write this down—'and He made seven." That was it! Those four words would serve as the title for our book.

As we began discussing the significance of the number six, my sister picked up the Bible and began reading in Genesis. We wanted to read about what had happened on the sixth day of creation.

Then God said, "Let us make man in our image,

*in our likeness, and let them rule over the fish of
the sea and the birds of the air, over the
livestock, over all the earth, and over all the
creatures that move along the ground." So God
created man in his own image, in the image of
God he created him; male and female he created
them* (Gen. 1:26, 27, NIV).

God gave us dominion over everything! In the
beginning He gave us power and authority over all the
earth, but when man sinned, he lost that dominion.
Again, through the death of Jesus on the cross and His
resurrection, we regained dominion over the earth, and it
is time for us to walk in the power and authority God
gave us.

Through that revelation, the name of our book
came about— *...and He made seven.* Tammy shared
with me that she'd had that revelation for awhile, but
Satan had made her feel that her idea was stupid, so she
had never shared her revelation before that time.

This book was birthed in prayer. May you, too,
reap the benefits of a bountiful prayer harvest.

Sharon Gooch
Shontelle Banks-Gossette
Tiffani McDonald

Section I

Darlene's TESTIMONIES

Thank You, Lord, for my deliverance...

From Fear to Freedom in Christ

Unless you have experienced living in a spiritual wasteland, you have no idea the weight of carrying such a heavy spiritual burden. I (Darlene) knew that Christ had died to set us free, and I desperately wanted to experience freedom in Him. The first four of my testimonies, which are interlinked, show, step-by-step, how the Lord brought me from life in a spiritual wilderness to a life of freedom in Him.

The Lord saved me when I was twelve years old, but I did not receive the baptism of the Holy Spirit. In the church where I grew up, what I understood about the Holy Spirit was that if you did not speak in other tongues you did not have the Holy Spirit. (See Acts 2:4 and 19:6.) Therefore, I had never received the baptism of the Holy Spirit because I never spoke with other tongues. I knew that I had received the Lord into my heart, but there was so much I did not understand. At age twenty I married, and I began attending church less and less. Five years later, my life would take a turn that would lead me further and further away from God.

When I was twenty-five years old, my mother died of cancer. After her death, I started down that wide path of destruction spoken of in Matthew 7:13, "Enter ye in at the strait gate: for wide is the gate, and broad is the way, that leadeth to destruction, and many there be which go in there at. . . . " The year following my mother's death, my pastor passed away also. I somehow lost control of my life, and those values that had once mattered in life had slipped from my reach.

I spent years doing my own thing, but I was constantly being tormented because I knew the life I was living was wrong. For many years I had been devastated by my mother's passing. I had a very hard time understanding why the Lord would take her from us. (Now that I know the Lord for myself, I know that no circumstances in life can defeat me because Jesus came to bring life. The Bible records in John 10:10, "The thief [Satan] cometh not, but for to steal, and to kill, and to destroy: I am come that they might have life, and that they might have it more abundantly.)"

When my pastor died, I remember saying, "Lord, who will preach me back to the altar?" Many years later when I was finally fed up with living life 'my way,' my sister invited me to the church that she attended—the church I would later join.

I repented of my sins and tried to live a saved life. I know it was the Lord that led me to my present church, Mt. Carmel, a predominantly black Pentecostal church in an urban setting. My pastor and his wife have been one of God's greatest blessings to me. Their teaching and their prayers have helped me to come to a greater knowledge of who I am in Christ today. I found myself continuously at the altar, even though I had always been afraid to approach the altar. I remember my pastor telling me once when I was in the prayer line that the Lord was going to use me as a conduit in bringing many people to God. (He spoke into my life, and now that word has become reality.)

Although I attended church regularly, and loved our services very much, I sensed that I was still missing out on something. I felt as though I were on the outside looking in. Sunday after Sunday, I watched others as they received their blessings—speaking in tongues, shouting and rejoicing in the holy dance, and praising God to the point where they did not care about what was going on around them. I wanted that experience too, but I did not know how to attain it. It was not that I had not been taught how to receive God's blessings; my problem was that I did not **do** what I was taught to do.

As much as I loved my church, for many years I still left there not getting the breakthrough I so desperately desired. I knew that the Holy Spirit was real in my life, but I had not yet spoken in tongues. I often entertained thoughts of leaving my church and going to a church I thought would not expect me to speak in tongues. (I know now that this was just a trick of the devil to keep me off focus. I had allowed Satan to use fear and doubt to stop the flow of my blessing.) I would fast, pray, and try to get into God's Word more. I stood in prayer line after prayer line for those things I thought I needed from God. I wanted to shout and dance in the holy dance. I wanted to speak in tongues. I wanted to be able to talk and testify in front of people without my voice quivering and knees shaking. I would leave church embarrassed because I thought I was not doing what I thought others thought I should have been doing.

I used to hate the times when visiting preachers or evangelists would come to run revivals. They would have 'Holy Ghost Night' and say words such as, "This is Holy Ghost Night," or "If you have never spoken in tongues before, make sure you come to the next service!" But as always, one more time I left service miserable, embarrassed, and disappointed. My pastor sometimes conducted this type of service, with many being saved and filled with the Holy Ghost. I hated it because I felt I was going to be put on the spot at the altar. I felt that everyone was watching me and nothing was happening. Most of the time I would return the next night, just in case that was really going to be my night to receive the blessing I so desperately wanted.

I remember trying to speak in tongues at home when I was alone or while riding alone in my car, but the sounds never came out right. I knew it was just self and not the Holy Spirit. I knew that the Word said we would speak in tongues as the Spirit gave us utterance (Act 2:4).

For many, many years I wandered in a spiritual wilderness from which there seemed no way to escape. The Holy Spirit always visited the services at Mt. Carmel, but, as always, I was the one looking around wishing He would visit me. Then one day before one of those 'Holy Ghost' nights, I whispered a prayer to the Lord, which went like this: "Lord, just give me enough to be able to claim without any doubt that I have received the Holy Ghost." That night, something happened to me. I cannot explain how it happened. I did not speak in tongues, but I knew without any doubt that I had received the Holy Ghost. (This happened at a church we were visiting.) I testified at my church the next Sunday that I had received the Holy Spirit. That is how I found out for myself that *you could* receive the Holy Spirit without speaking in tongues at the same time.

I know that speaking in tongues is evidence of one having received the Holy Spirit according to the Scripture: "And when Paul had laid his hands upon them, the Holy Ghost came on them; and they spake with with tongues, and prophesied" (Acts 19:6). Yet I knew that I had received the Holy Spirit in my heart. Although I did not speak in tongues for years, no one could tell me I did not have the Holy Spirit. I know without any doubt that I had received Him into my heart. The Lord made certain of that because of the small prayer I prayed before Holy Ghost night.

If you are seeking the baptism of the Holy Spirit, my advice to you would be to ask God for the evidence of speaking in tongues immediately. Because I did not speak in tongues immediately, I allowed Satan to build the strongholds of fear and doubt in my life. I was saved and filled with the Holy Spirit, but I was not *free.* I do not know how or why *not* speaking in tongues would give Satan such a stronghold on my life, but it did. But, by the grace of God, I was emerging out of a spiritual wilderness that had prevented my experiencing a life of freedom in Christ.

Through different experiences with Him, God has allowed me to break free of some of the shackles which held me captive in the wilderness, but I had yet to face some giants before I reached my land of Canaan. For some strange reason I was plagued by the phobia that people were always watching me; therefore, I could never just be myself. I could never praise the Lord with all my heart for thinking that others were watching me. I knew without a doubt, however, that, like Caleb, I would conquer this mountain.

Healing Miracle

One day I found myself needing God more than ever before. In January of 1998, I was standing in my bedroom in front of the mirror applying deodorant when I touched a sore spot that caused me to say, "OUCH!" Then I felt under my arm, and surely enough, I discovered a very sore spot. Knowing there was a history of cancer on my mother's side of the family, the first thought that came to my mind was that I had cancer. Immediately after that thought, I said, "No, Satan, you are a liar! By the strips of my Savior Jesus Christ, I am healed" (Is.53:5). At that point I began talking to the Lord: "Lord, I know Your Word is true, and I am going to stand on your Word."

I said to myself that I would wait a couple of weeks and see if the soreness would leave. During that time, rarely did I even think about what I had discovered earlier. God had already prepared me to stand on His Word. After a couple of weeks had gone by, I felt in the same area and noticed that my underarm was still very sore. At that time I scheduled an appointment for a mammogram. I told the Lord that I did not care what the doctor's report said. I would continue to believe His report—that by His stripes I was healed. I went to have the mammogram and was told I would receive a copy of the results in a few weeks.

I went on with my life, seldom thinking about the test. Occasionally, when the devil would try to torment me, I would immediately call him a liar and go on my way. When the test results finally came in the mail, I was a little surprised because most of the time the test results had been the farthest thing from my mind. The results of the test indicated an abnormality in my right breast and that I should come in for further testing. I was not moved by the results because I knew in my heart that Jesus had suffered and died on the cross for my healing, which meant I was healed of cancer.

I made an appointment for more testing. I was told again I would receive the results in the mail in a few weeks. I continued to live my life the same as always, seldom giving any thought of receiving the results. When the results came for the second time, again I was surprised because I had forgotten about it. This time the results said I should come in for a biopsy. I called my doctor to see if he had received the results of my test. He had, and he made arrangements for me to see the surgeon who would perform the biopsy. The surgeon called me to his office after receiving the results.

I had already told my husband, sister, daughter, son, and nieces about having to go for a biopsy. Of course, my niece Mashan would be the one to accompany me to the surgeon's office. She worked nights, and everyone else worked days, so she was with me all the time. I thank God for my family, for it is another one of God's greatest blessings to me. They were concerned about me, but I assured them that "Satan is a liar, and I am healed."

After Mashan and I were seated, the surgeon told us the news. The biopsy revealed that the tumor was malignant. I did not say a word; neither did I show any emotion. The doctor continued talking, making every attempt to console me, I guess. I do not remember all that he said. His voice seemed to be coming from a distance. The only thing on my mind was that my family would have to be told the results. I knew they would take the news very hard because we all knew cancer ran in our family. The idea of having to tell my family about my condition saddened me. I knew they would think I was going to die of cancer, but I knew that this was not true. The surgeon noticed a lone teardrop roll down my cheek, but that tear was for my family, not for myself. I knew without a doubt that I was healed. He continued to explain the two surgeries I would need to rid my body of cancer.

As Mashan and I prepared to leave the office, the surgeon said to me, "You're a very strong woman." My response was, "That's because my faith is in God." The only answer I would accept in my life was that I was healed. Later, when I told my family what the doctor had said, I found that they were all in agreement with me—Sharon, Mashan, Tammy, Tiffani, and my daughter, Shontelle, all believing God and standing on His Word for the manifestation of my healing. What a great joy my family was to me! I said a prayer to the Lord, asking Him to prevent my breast from being removed and to keep me from chemotherapy.

Several of my family members were with me during the surgeries, but two of my brothers were not there. I did not tell them about my condition because I knew they did not have the level of faith that the rest of us had, and I knew that, no matter what I said, they would still be very worried and upset. (I believe as we write our testimonies, the Lord is going to do great things in their lives.)

I arranged to consult with the oncologist, who would prescribe post-operative treatments for me. He told me I would have six weeks of radiation therapy. As he explained the procedure to me, he asked me if I knew what half a centimeter was. When I said no, he demonstrated the size with his finger. It looked to be no larger than one-forth inch. He said, "I don't know how that small amount of cancer was ever detected, unless it was God." He explained two other possibilities, but all I remembered him saying was "unless it was God." I shook my head in agreement with him.

Later, the six of us began to declare, in the Name of Jesus, that the curse of cancer and every disease was broken off our family. I knew in my heart that He is my healer, according to Ps. 103:3b: "Who forgiveth all thine iniquities; who healeth all thy diseases. . . ." I had taken one small phrase from the Bible to sustain me, "by His stripes I am healed," (Is.53:5). I stood on that Word and that Word healed me.

Strongholds Cast Down

What I am about to share with you played a very large part in my receiving total deliverance from all the weights holding me bound. Even though I was singing about being free, I had never known how it felt to be truly free. Somewhere in the back of my mind, I had this fear of not wanting to do, or thinking God would have me doing something I did not want to do. Therefore, I was never honest about saying yes to the will of God. This became another one of Satan's strongholds in my life.

Believers often talk and sing about being totally surrendered to God, but in reality, we are not. It was not until I had acknowledged that I had not completely surrendered my heart to the Lord that I was in the position for deliverance. Only then did God reveal to me what was holding me back. It had taken me most of my life to make that discovery. In times past, when I had said, "Lord, whatever you want me to do, I'll do it," this was not completely true. I thought I had really meant it, but God revealed the truth to me: I had been fooling myself, but God knew the truth; He knew that I hadn't totally surrendered my heart to Him.

I was aware that I was fearful of talking in front of people, but I did not associate this fear with being totally surrendered. I was not even aware that my failure to surrender was holding back my blessings. But I thank God that He revealed this truth to me. I found myself on my knees crying out to the Lord, saying, "Lord, I know I'm free because your Word says I'm free, but Lord, I want to feel free!" I cried out to God for His Word to come alive in me. The apostle Paul's message to the saints at Galatia was addressed to me, too: "Stand fast therefore in the liberty wherewith Christ hath made us free, and be not entangled again with the yoke of bondage" (Gal. 5:1).

Why had I waited so long to ask God to allow me to feel free? I was hung up on the verse in the Bible that says, ". . . The just shall live by faith" (Rom. 1:17). I had never thought of asking God for the faith to feel free. I just thought I had to have the faith in me to be free. I had already experienced so many spiritual disappointments in the past that I did not realize my level of expectation had reached such depth. There were times when I left church services, crying and not understanding why I could never receive the blessings I wanted from God.

Surrender of the Heart

After all the spiritual anguish I had suffered, I was desperate for a move of God in my life. My breakthrough finally came one Thursday night during our monthly Women of Excellence service (WOE) at Mt. Carmel, conducted by the first lady (pastor's wife) of our church. I remember so well raising my arms to the Lord and saying with all my heart, "Lord, I surrender my all to you." For the first time in my life, I meant every word. No matter what I may have to do, I felt in my heart that God was all I needed.

There was a time during my wilderness experience that I had heard the voice of the Lord say, "Just as I suffered and died on the cross for your salvation and healing, I also suffered and died so that you would be free." I told the Lord that His suffering and dying on the cross would not be in vain for me. God did not wait for me to do anything else before He started pulling down those strongholds. All He had been waiting for was for me to truly believe in my heart. One day I found myself walking around in my house saying, "I'm free, I'm free! I'm really, really FREE!" I knew without a doubt that God had set me free. I would never be in that type of bondage ever again. Praise our God! Hallelujah!

The Lord filled me with so much faith and love for Him. I was no longer on the outside looking in; now I felt on the inside with God. (I am so glad I did not leave Mt. Carmel. I know my pastor and wife's prayers for me year after year had played a vital role in bringing me to my point of deliverance.) I found myself coming to church and praising God without thinking of anyone else but Him. I could praise Him in whatever way I wanted to without worrying about what other people thought. I even began to stammer as I went forth in praise to God. I was so glad that the Word, as prophesied by the prophet Isaiah, had become a reality in my life: "For with stammering lips and another tongue will he speak to this people" (Is. 28:11). Shortly afterward, I began to speak in tongues as the Spirit gave me utterance, according to the Pentecostal experience recorded in Acts 2:4: "And they were all filled with the Holy Ghost, and began to speak with other tongues, as the Spirit gave them utterance." I knew that the Lord had, indeed, set me free from the fear of people.

My life had taken a new direction, and my heart was open to whatever God had for me to do. One day I was reading my Bible and the Lord took me to the eighth chapter of Deuteronomy, verses 2-7, 15-16, 18-19. As I read, I understood why the Spirit had led me to this chapter.

> .....[2] *And thou shalt remember all the way which the LORD thy God led thee these forty years in the wilderness, to humble thee, and to prove thee, to know what was in thine heart, whether thou wouldest keep his commandments, or no. [3] And he humbled thee, and suffered thee to hunger, and fed thee with manna, which thou knewest not, neither did thy fathers know; that he might make thee know that man doth not live by bread only, but by every word that proceedeth out of the mouth of the LORD doth man live. [4] Thy raiment waxed not old upon thee, neither did thy foot swell, these forty years. [5] Thou shalt also consider in thine heart, that, as a man chasteneth his son, so the LORD thy God chasteneth thee. [6] Therefore thou shalt keep the commandments of*

the LORD thy God, to walk in his ways, and to fear him. [7] For the LORD thy God bringeth thee into a good land, a land of brooks of water, of fountains and depths that spring out of valleys and hills . . . . [15] Who led thee through that great and terrible wilderness, wherein were fiery serpents, and scorpions, and drought, where there was no water; who brought thee forth water out of the rock of flint; [16] Who fed thee in the wilderness with manna, which thy fathers knew not, that he might humble thee, and that he might prove thee, to do thee good at thy latter end. . . [18] But thou shalt remember the LORD thy God: for it is he that giveth thee power to get wealth, that he may establish his covenant which he sware unto thy fathers, as it is this day. [19] And it shall be, if thou do at all forget the Lord thy God, and walk after other gods, and serve them, and worship them, I testify against you this day that ye shall surely perish. . . ."

Like Israel, I had suffered the consequences of disobedience in the past, and God had taken care of me; but I felt that God was saying something more. This chapter spoke, not only to the Israelites' past but also to their future. God was speaking to my future also! He was saying, "Darlene, there are some consequences to disobedience. Do not fall prey to the temptation of prosperity, and above all, do not turn away from following the one and only true God."

Not long after God had spoken to me through His Word, my daughter, Shontelle, shared a vision God had shown her. A few months later, one of my nieces,

Tiffani, experienced a similar divine visitation. Her vision was a confirmation of what God had shown her cousin Shontelle . This encounter with God marked the beginning of a new spiritual walk with God for all of us. God would take the six of us, step-by-step, to a new level in Him.

Drug House Closed

We did not go into this circle of prayer ignorant of the enemy's ways. We were very much aware that Satan would be angry, and that he would engage us in spiritual warfare. However, we also know who was on our side—an awesome God—and we would have the victory. It seemed as though the devil came at us in all his strength; we went through things we thought we would never have to go through. We were confident, however, that God would hear us when we cried out to Him, for the Word records: "The righteous cry and the LORD heareth, and delivereth them out of all their troubles" (Ps. 34:17). One request we had before the Lord involved our neighborhood.

There was a drug house right next door to my house. We had always prayed that the Lord would remove the drugs and save the drug dealer who lived there. We did not want to see him hurt or killed. We just wanted our neighborhood free of drugs.

As I was standing in my front door one day, I watched as the police came and took the dealer away. The police had found him sitting outside his house in a stolen car. They did not enter the house. When I called my daughter, sister, and nieces and told them what had happened, we all praised God. Even though the dealer was gone, we continued to pray for him. After all, we knew the Lord loved him as much as He loved us. We prayed especially for his salvation. I said to myself, that he should be gone for a long time. How wrong I was!

Less than three weeks later, the same drug dealer was back in business in the same house. The noise and traffic in the wee hours of the morning started again. This was a let down, but we continued to pray. This temporary setback would not shake our confidence in God. We stood on I John 5:14,15, which says, "And this is the confidence that we have in him, that, if we ask anything according to his will, he heareth us. And if we know that he hear us, whatever we ask, we know that we have the petitions that we desired of him."

Then Satan tried to discourage us even more. The same drug dealer in the house right next to us opened another drug house next door to his house. We were not ignorant of Satan's strategies, so we continued to pray and thank God, because we knew that He heard our prayers. The police raided the second drug house and took the drug dealer away a second time. But this time, the events that followed were different. The second house caught fire, and was rendered inhabitable. Later it was boarded up and condemned. The house next door to me was also boarded up and condemned. (Both houses have since been demolished.)

We did not see the drug dealer for months. I knew he was incarcerated, but I did not know for how long. We just praised God because the noise, the traffic, the gunfire and all the other dangers associated with drug houses were no longer there to annoy us.(I praise God even now as I sit here writing.)

One day there was a knock at my door, and I was at home alone. I looked out and, to my surprise, I saw the drug dealer at my door. I opened the door because I know the young man, and I cared about him. He had come to apologize to me for his behavior. He said, "I'm sorry I had a drug house next door to you. I'm through with drugs. I know I'm called to be a preacher." I do not remember what I said to the young man, but I am glad that God had us praying for him. Sometimes we still see that same young man on the street corners, but I pray that God's will be done in his life. Amen. Although the main focus of our prayer circle was not drug houses, I shared this story to show you how awesome God is, and to show that He cares about everyone.

Drawing Closer in Prayer

Although we continued to pray for ourselves, our prayers were centered on the men in our family—sons, grandsons, husbands, fathers, brothers, uncles, cousins and nephews. Satan had launched an all-out war against the men in our family. It seemed as though Satan was hitting us where it hurt the most—our sons, our hearts. I cannot go into detail about my son's unfortunate circumstances. I can only say that my heart aches for him. Even knowing that God is going to work everything out, it is hard for a mother to see her son hurting. Not only were our sons under attack, but the rest of the men also faced their unique spiritual battles.

One night we had gathered at Mashan's house for prayer as usual, but that night became one of our most memorable. We were all going through heartaches with sons, grandsons, or husbands. After prayer, while we were listening to a song entitled "It's Only a Test," we stood in a circle holding hands, tears streaming from our eyes. As the words of the song penetrated our hearts, we pulled into a tighter circle and just clung to one another. It seemed as though we could feel one another's pain, and somehow we bonded even closer than we had already been. Somehow we knew that the spiritual bonding brought about through God that night would play an important part in tearing Satan's kingdom down. Glory Hallelujah! We cried, but we rejoiced, knowing we had the victory over Satan—the **Blood-bought Victory**!

My Husband's Prayer

My husband is an extraordinary man. In the thirty-three years we have been married, he has always been dedicated and committed entirely to the well being of our family. He has always believed in God. Although he was brought up in the Baptist church with his mother and the rest of the family, he was not a churchgoer when we married.

Many times when we would have family gatherings on holidays, my husband would be the first person to say, "Let us all hold hands and pray." That year my sister, Sharon, had invited the family to her house for Memorial Day. Because of my son's situation, I was somewhat apprehensive about how things would work out. I said a prayer to the Lord and asked Him for peace and harmony so that my son and his family would just enjoy our family gathering. I prayed that everyone would get along and there would be no more animosity among family members.

The day I prayed that prayer just happened to be the day the six of us gathered for prayer at my house. I asked my husband if he wanted to join us. Right before we started prayer, some more of my family stopped by. My husband came into the room and said, "Let us all hold hands and pray together."

This is my recollection, with the help of my niece Tammy, of what my husband said in that prayer: "This is for me, Jesus. Remove the fear. I know you can do it. Without You, we are nothing. Help us to love; help us to fulfill our purpose."

Thank you, Jesus! Thank you for choosing us. Please help us to stay together.

A Prayer That Touched My Heart

On one of our prayer nights, I remember Mashan saying a special prayer for my son. She asked the Lord to fix her heart so that she would not hold a grudge against an individual with ties to him. She told the Lord that she was willing to do anything He wanted her to do to help rid her of the animosity she felt against this person. She told us before we started prayer that she and my son had engaged in a long talk. She said that she could see the hurt and the pain in his eyes. My niece Tammy concluded that the only way for us to reach the other person was for us to allow the light of Jesus to shine through us.

The day after Memorial Day, I received a telephone call from my niece Tiffani. She asked me if I had been praying for her. I told her that I had prayed for peace and harmony at our Memorial Day gathering. She acknowledged that someone must have been praying for her because she did not feel anything negative at all for anyone. The Lord had answered my prayer once again. At the gathering, everyone had had a wonderful time, laughing and talking, and enjoying the food. When I looked at my son, I could tell that a heavy burden had been lifted off his shoulders.

God is so much more than any words man could ever begin to express. He is El-Shaddai, *God of more than enough.* He is everything to me.

One day when the family just happened to gather at my house, we started talking about all of us going to church together on Sunday. Different ones were saying, "If you go, I'll go," and in return someone would say, "If you go, I'll go." One of my unspoken prayers had always been that the Lord would bring my family to church together, worshipping and praising Him. That next Sunday my husband, children, grandchildren, nieces, nephews, my brother Thomas and his wife and family, all showed up at church. Praise God for answered prayer! My cup runneth over!

Financial Blessing

In March of 1999, my husband received a check in the mail, one with figures larger than we had ever seen addressed to us. We had not borrowed the money, so we knew we did not have to pay it back. This money was a financial blessing from the Lord, one which would completely get us out of debt. When we received the check, I was the first to see it because my husband was at work. I did not even call him. He would have the surprise of his life when he returned home. I just began to praise God.

Even though our children were grown and had jobs, they were still experiencing financial problems. Through our blessing, God would allow us to be a blessing to them. We had always wanted to help them financially, but my husband and I just did not have the money. All we could do was to let them move back in with us until they were able to move out again.

When my husband and I sat down with the check, the amount was so large that it was just hard for us to believe what we were seeing. Right away, he began making a list of what we were going to do with the money. I knew that the first thing on the list should have been tithes, but it was not. I did not say anything to him about tithes at that time. I already knew his views on that. If you cannot pay your bills, how can you pay tithes? So I just paid tithes on whatever he would give me. My husband started the list out with our children. I was very thankful to God for allowing us to be a financial blessing to them. It felt so good to be able to help them in that way.

It was not very long before we were right back in the same financial bind we had been before we received the check. I knew it was coming because God should have been first on that list. (This is a good time to tell you about my tithing dilemma.)

When I was working, I would pay tithes, but most of the time it would be after the bills had been paid. When my job laid me off, I would give whatever I could, or whatever money I had in my purse at the time. For a long time, I struggled with whether or not I should just go ahead and tithe on my husband's check. We seemed to stay in financial difficulty. When it seemed as if we were pulling out, something would pull us right back down again. After a few years of my not working —and not ever wanting to work again—I made a decision that I know came from the Lord.

I thought to myself, "The Lord sees us as one—what is his is mine, and what is mine is his." Since my husband always let me take care of the bills and checkbook, I could just subtract tithes from his check and not even include that ten percent in my checkbook. I began writing a check every week off the top and putting God first, and my husband never new the difference. He would ask me how much money we had in the bank, and I would tell him. I made another change in my spending habits. I stopped writing checks for things I really could do without.

Within a few months, our checkbook started looking better and better. I knew that if I started putting God first He would reward us. I had been claiming for a long time that someday we would be able to own cars and houses which we had paid for in cash. When my husband retired in July of 2002, we were blessed to buy a brand new Sport Utility Vehicle with cash, paid off the mortgage on our house and all our other bills. Now we were debt free. (I am not saying this is the way you should take care of your tithes. All I know is that when I decided to put God first, we began to receive more and more of His blessings.

The Lawsuit

Early in 2001, my husband and I received a letter in the mail stating that we were bring sued by the credit union of the company for which he had worked. The lawsuit was for several thousand dollars. Both our hearts just dropped at the thought of another money problem for us to worry about. The reason we were being sued was that my husband had co-signed for a car that someone very dear to us had traded for a different car without our knowledge. We knew we would need a lawyer, so I began my search.

At our family prayer that week, I told all my prayer partners about the lawsuit. We took it down in prayer every time our prayer group came together. I found a lawyer and faxed him all the papers pertaining to the lawsuit. It seemed as though it took forever for the wheels to begin to turn. Every now and then we would receive letters from the lawyer concerning calls that he had to make or people he had to see regarding our case.

One day while I was watching one of my favorite Christian programs on television, the pastor was speaking on asking the Lord to bring closure to different hindrances concerning the saints. He even mentioned pending lawsuits. When the six of us came together for prayer, we agreed on closure to the lawsuit in our favor immediately so that my husband and I would not be required to pay the credit union anything.

In July I received a call from my lawyer telling me that the case between my husband and the credit union had been dismissed in our favor, and we did not have to pay them anything. He said we would receive the papers in the mail releasing us of all obligations to the credit union. Of course, we all rejoiced, giving glory to God for lifting the heavy burden off our shoulders.

Then the bill from the lawyer came. It was rather large, but, compared to what we were being sued for, we counted it as small. The law firm was very considerate, and allowed us to pay the bill in small monthly payments. My husband, knowing what the Lord had done for us, got up the next Sunday morning and went to the eight o'clock service. All I can say is what an awesome God we serve. Why would anyone want to live life without our God?

Prayers of Faith

After the Lord delivered us from the lawsuit, I heard Him say, "Start writing the answers to your prayers." (God was showing me that we do not have to wait to see the manifestation of answers to the prayers we pray. The key was to have faith in Him.) Although there were many prayers I had prayed for which I had not seen an answer in the natural, I knew that those prayers had reached heaven and would be answered. I picked up my notebook and began to write the *anticipated answers* to my prayers.

This is how I see the answers to the prayers we have been bringing before the Lord:

My Daughter, Shontelle

I envision my daughter successful, both naturally and spiritually. I thank You, Lord, that she is married to a wonderful, saved, sanctified, Holy Spirit-filled man who loves her as Christ loves the church, and her children as his own. She owns a successful business, but she does not have to be there to run it. A saved staff keeps the business running smoothly. She is living in the home of more than her dreams. She has her own ministry in the church with her husband and children. They are rich spiritually, financially and in every way. There is no more fear from Satan in their lives.

She is saved, sanctified, and filled with the Holy Ghost and fire. She feels free and is fulfilling God's purpose in her life. Her entire family always puts God first, seeks His face, and loves Him. They give Him all the glory, praise and honor for what He has done in their lives.

My Son and His Family

By faith, I am believing this blessed life for my son and his family: The Lord has saved my son and his wife, and they are bringing up their children in the church. The children are saved and being taught to love and obey God. My son, too, owns his own business and is doing well. Within a very short time, he became a millionaire. He loves the Lord and he and his family worship God together with us at church. He is so much into God that it is almost unbelievable. But God is a good God. He is faithful; He is El-Shaddai—*God of more than enough.* My son and his family are also active in the ministry together, doing God's will. They have a beautiful home and have put God first in everything they do. They are very blessed and are a blessing to many others.

Thank You, Lord, with all my heart. My children are all healthy. They give God all the honor, praise, and glory for what He has done for them. They have the victory and the favor of God our Father. All of my children and grandchildren are saved, sanctified and filled with the Holy Ghost and that with fire, and are bringing glory and honor to God. What a blessing!

Sharon and Her Husband

Father, I thank you for allowing my sister the opportunity to retire early. I thank you for her and her husband's finances being more than enough to accomplish all that You want them to do and to bless all those whom You want them to bless. Thank you for their being debt-free and living out Your purpose in their lives, and just for being able to do all the things they have wanted to do in life. Thank You, Lord, for their good health and for longevity of life. Thank You for a happy, peaceful, fruitful, and prosperous life together in You, Lord. Thank You for all the blessings and miracles You have given them. Amen.

Mashan and Her Family

Lord, I thank You so much for all You have done for Mashan and her three sons. I thank You, Lord, for how You have not only made them rich in their finances, but You have also made them rich in You. Mashan had always said that she would be in full time ministry for You. No one could have ever dreamed of what You have done with her and her sons. They are all living for You and doing Your will. Their purpose in life is to serve, love, and obey You. I thank You, Lord, for my niece and her sons. I thank You for her mother's salvation, healing, and deliverance. I thank You for every miracle and every blessing You have bestowed upon them. I am in awe of all that You have done for us and our families. Thank You for opening doors. Thank You for seeing us through. Lord, we praise You for Your goodness and Your mercy toward our family.

My NieceTammy

Father, thank You for the call on Tammy's life to become a missionary. Thank You for allowing her to hear and obey your call. Now she has an international ministry, speaking all over the world, building up Your Kingdom and tearing Satan's kingdom down. She is in demand for speaking engagements everywhere because of the great anointing You have placed on her life.

Thank You for giving her a husband who loves her and her children very much. Thank you for her business that has become very prosperous. Thank You, Lord, for Cortney's healing and Carlin's life in the ministry of God. Amen.

My Niece Tiffani

Father, I thank You for keeping Tiffani's family together. I thank You for how You have taught her and her husband to love and cherish each other. I thank You, Lord, that they are godly parents, teaching their children values and bringing them up in the way of the Lord.

Thank You, Lord, that they are free of debt and are living the good life. Nothing is lacking. Thank You, Lord, for Your faithfulness. Thank You for giving them long life, peace, strength, love, good health, happiness, and prosperity in every way of life. We love You, Lord.

My Brothers and the Extended Family

Father, I truly thankYou for the salvation of our brothers and their families. I also thank You, Lord, for the salvation of my cousins and their families. Lord, I thank you for how You have just brought all of us out of debt. Thank You, Lord, for opening our eyes to see Your Glorious Light in the face of Jesus Christ, our Lord.

Lord I knew that You would save my brothers and the rest of my family, and make everything right. Thank You for Your healing in all of them. Thank You for long, fruitful, peaceful, and prosperous lives that continue to be on fire for You. Thank You, Lord, for being our El-Shaddai, and for being all that You are to us and in us. We love You. Thank You, Lord, for making known Your purpose for each one of them. Father, grant them the strength and courage to fulfill Your will and purpose for their lives. Amen.

My Husband and Me (Darlene)

Lord, I thank You that my husband has brought many people to the Lord. He attends church all the time. You have given my husband and me a place in ministry, and we are striving with all our hearts to do Your will. The ministry You have given us is more than we could have ever imagined. People are being saved, healed, delivered, and made whole in every way possible. By the hundreds of thousands, they are being made rich both spiritually as well as financially. We praise You, Lord!

My family lives in a new house, one which has everything I ever wanted in a home, and so much more. It has large, beautiful, safe windows that I can open anytime to allow a cool, soft breeze to blow throughout. Every room is spacious; there is a place and a space for everything. My husband even has a pond at the edge of the back yard. We are living debt free, and have more than enough money to fulfill our every dream. We have been a huge blessing to our family, our church (Mt. Carmel), and to everyone else the Lord sends our way.

Our desire is to go higher and higher in You, God. We want to know You—to know Your heart. Lord, I want this for all members of my family and friends, and for my church family. Lord, I would like to be able to help my community; by eliminating the bad elements so that my community will be a pleasant and pretty place in which to live. Father, I thank you for all these things, in the Name of Jesus.

Our book has been published and has sold millions of copies. People are being saved, healed, and delivered immediately as they read the book.

All of the members of my family arc alive and well, living for God, and fulfilling their purposes in God. El-Shaddai!

My New Home

I declare, in the Name of Jesus, that I am moving from my present home into another home which we will pay for in cash. My family and I have lived in the same house for thirty years, and I have wanted to move for more years than I can remember. The house was already thirty years old when we purchased it. I take a stand on

God's Word and declare that God will bless me with a new home while I still have time to enjoy it and take care of it.

For several years now I have been claiming my new house, and I will continue to proclaim it. I know that the Lord is teaching me patience. He is teaching me how to be still and know that He is God. He is teaching me to stand on His Word, no matter how long it takes. He is teaching me that not only did He suffer and die on the cross for my sins, my healing, and my deliverance, but He also suffered and died so that I could have abundant life. I claim the abundant life, in Jesus' Name! Hallelujah!

The Book Mashan Gave Me

When Mashan handed me a book to read, entitled T*he Walk of the Spirit, the Walk of Power,* by Dave Roberson, I had no idea how this book would change my life. One of Mashan's friends had given it to her to read, but she wanted me to read it first and give her my opinion.

I began to read the book and cried all the way through the first few pages. Then I came to some parts where I said to myself, "I have heard all this before," so I put the book down. Some time went by before I picked up the book and began to read again. It was becoming a little more interesting, but I read only a few pages and put it down again. I am not sure how much time went by before I picked the book up again, but when I did, I could not put it down. I read until I was just too tired to read any more. From then on, I read it at every opportunity. By the time I finished the book, I knew God had taken me to a higher place in Him.

When I started reading *The Walk of the Spirit*, my prayer language had been nothing more than stammering, but by the time I finished reading it, there was a new anointing upon me. I was speaking in tongues as the Spirit gave me utterance everyday. I even felt different.I told Mashan that it was a good book, and that she should read it. She did not start reading it right away, so I told her to give it to Sharon to read. In talking with Mashan's friend about the book, Sharon was told the book had an anointing on it. I told Sharon I was very much aware of this. She began to read the book and enjoyed it.

I believe if all of us in our prayer circle will read *The Walk of the Spirit*, all six of us will experience a greater anointing. I thank God for the friend who put that book into our hands. Reading other books, in addition to reading the Bible, has given us more insight and a greater understanding of spiritual things. Of course, the Bible, God's Word, is supreme and foremost in having a closer relationship with the Lord, but we have found other sources extremely beneficial. A better understanding of God and what He desires to do through us has increased our anointing.

The Bloodline

The Lord has brought me a long way in my prayer life. There were times when the six of us came together for prayer that my mind would wander, and I would be thinking of other things. I remember one night I heard Tammy say, "It's all about You, Lord," and her words brought my heart and mind back to praising God. Even though I knew everything was all about Him, I sensed in my heart that God wanted to show me more about why "it was all about Him." Understanding the real truth behind what Tammy had said began with my admitting that sometimes I had been selfish in my just thinking and praying about things I wanted God to do for me.

One morning as I turned on gospel music to usher in the Holy Spirit so that I could spend time with the Lord while I was at home alone, something very awesome happened. Just as the music began to play, I began to pray in my prayer language. While I was praising Him in my prayer language, the Lord began to show me something awesome. I could see the pain and agony of Jesus' crucifixion. As I prayed, I could see the terrible things Jesus suffered as He was being crucified. I could see the nails being driven into His hands and His feet. Then the Lord took me back to the Garden of Gethsemane, where He was praying before His crucifixion. I could see the large drops of blood falling from His face. As I continued to watch this scene, I heard the Lord say, **"This is why it's all about Me."**

That day I discovered what it means to wail before God. I was praying in tongues and moaning loudly at the same time. The kinds of sound coming from my mouth must have been what the Bible calls *wailing*. It was as if I were there kneeling before the cross and watching Him give His life for me. I could hardly contain myself.

A few weeks later, one Tuesday night after our family prayer, God showed Tiffani another vision. She told me the Lord showed me running around my house three times, but He did not reveal to her why I was running. She told me that I would have to ask God for the meaning of this vision. I did not question her, for I knew what she had told me had come from God, and I would obey Him.

Early the next morning, I ran around my house three times. When I finished I said, "I surely am glad He said three times and not seven." Although doing three laps had been hard, I would have done seven if He had demanded that of me, for the Word says, "I can do all things through Christ who strengthens me" (Phil. 4:13).

As I was running up the steps to the front porch, I was so tired I stumbled on the steps and almost fell through the screen door. I asked the Lord to reveal to me what this vision meant. Later that morning, on a television ministry program I was watching, the host and her guests were discussing God's divine protection. They were talking about how they had driven around their children's school three times and prayed to draw, or mark, the bloodline of Jesus around that school. I said to myself, "What God was doing earlier this morning was drawing the bloodline of Jesus around my house." Praise God! I was so happy that the precious blood that Jesus shed for me on the cross at Calvary was the same blood that was surrounding my house, creating the bloodline of Jesus. The blood of Jesus could secure my family like no other security system could ever do.

Later that day, as I was returning from running an errand, I saw two ambulances, a fire truck, and police cars all over the place. Uniformed policemen and detectives were milling around the area. I saw a couple of paramedics loading one person into an ambulance.

Then I saw what I thought was a body in a body bag lying in the yard. I went out the back door to get a closer look. By this time television cameramen were on the scene. I overheard a man walking down the street say, "Two of them were shot." That very day two people were shot and killed at a house behind mine. I was certainly glad that "No weapon formed against us shall prosper. . ." (Isaiah 54:17).

Sometimes the things God has us do—such as running around the house three times— may sound silly to us, but we must come to the knowledge that there is a reason for everything God commands us to do. When we obey Him, we are blessed by our obedience.

All I Had To Do Was 'Say It'

At this time in my life, one of my brothers had come to live with us because he and his wife were having marital problems. My daughter, son, and grandson had already moved back home because of their financial situations. My house was full. People had begun to get on my nerves, mainly my brother, whom I love dearly.

I found myself involved in the conflict between my brother and his estranged wife. I became the messenger for both my brother and his wife. She would call me with messages for my brother, and I would tell her to tell him herself. Then he would tell me that if she called to tell her this and that. I would tell both of them that I was not telling anyone anything—that I was not the go-between in their disputes.

I was recovering from surgery and had not long been released from the hospital. My brother began getting sick, and I was taking him back and forth to the hospital. He had to have surgery, and my sister and I tried to be with him as much as we could. One day he became so sick that I had to take him back to the hospital. This time, however, I just dropped him off and went back home. As I was driving home I said to myself, "When I get home I'm going to take a sleeping pill and sleep until time to go to church." This was the day of our once-a-month Women of Excellence service.

When I arrived home, everyone else had gone to work. I sat on my sofa, and the Holy Spirit began to speak to me. The next thing I knew, I was walking through my house reading and speaking forth the Word of God. I knew without a doubt that I was punching Satan out left and right. I continued to read the Scriptures and repeat God's Word back to Him. God was declaring His promises to me and to all who love Him and put Him first in their lives. I sat down on the sofa again, and I heard the Lord say, "All you had to do was say it; the battle is Mine, not yours!" I just began to praise God. At the time I didn't know it, but God had taken me to a new level in Him.

I went to church that night and testified of all these things. This was the first time I had no fear as I stood before the congregation; neither did my voice shake. I had received a Word from God that day, and He gave me all the boldness I needed to give my testimony. As a matter of fact, as soon as the first lady asked for someone to testify, I immediately arose from my seat, went to the front of the church, and with holy boldness I began to give my testimony.

I knew that I could take no credit. I understood clearly the psalmist's words: "This is the LORD's doing; it is marvelous in our eyes" (Ps. 118:23).

After my brother had lived with me for a year, the Lord blessed him with a large rental house. There was room enough for his three children to visit him and stay over. Both my brother and I were very happy that he was on his own again.

It's in His Name!

During one of our monthly Women of Excellence services, once again I was in the prayer line, and our first lady laid hands on me. She said, "Darlene, there's a stronghold, but I see it being broken. The Lord said, 'It's in His Name... it's in His Name.'" She said I would have to seek God for the meaning.

Later at home I asked the Lord what He meant by saying 'It's in His Name.' I had no idea. Suddenly it hit me! I had not really been doing everything the Lord wanted me to do. I knew that I should be laying hands on the sick and declaring them healed in Jesus' Name. My pastor had always said that what God does for you, He will do through you. Ever since the Lord had healed me of cancer I knew I should lay hands on the sick because His Word says that ". . . they shall lay hands on the sick, and they shall recover" (Mark 16:18b). This meant every believer. I came to the realization that I had a fear of laying hands on people in church. I had laid hands on my family members, and sometimes on friends also, but doing this in church was something I did not do. The next series of events will help explain my fear.

When my sister Sharon's lifelong friend, whom I knew also, was diagnosed with cancer, diabetes, and other illnesses, my sister asked me to go with her to pray for her friend. We both prayed, and I shared with her how the Lord had healed me of cancer. I told her that He would do the same for her. We had printed and cut our Scriptures on healing and taped them around her apartment to encourage her. She knew that God was a healer, but she had not been taught that God would heal her. We prayed with her many times, but she seemed to worsen. I truly thought the Lord would heal her, but in a few months she died.

Her death was the stumbling block that I had never been able to overcome. When I talked to the first lady about it, one of the things she said to me was "God has the last word." I had thought that my hands were not anointed enough to heal—or something stupid like that. But the Holy Spirit, through our first lady, reminded me that I can do nothing on my own. I understood that there was no need to be afraid because I had no power to heal; God is the healer. My job was to pray according to the Scriptures and believe to see the manifestation of healing. It is in the name of Jesus that deliverance comes. I believe that was what God was telling me. Healing did not come from me; nor is there healing in any other name other than the name of Jesus. The battle is His and not mine. All you or I have to do is *say it* and then believe it.

Holy Ghost Night Revisited

On Wednesday night, our church has what we call 'Family Night.' We gather for dinner at five o'clock in the evening. The next hour, from six to seven o'clock, is devoted to prayer and worship. From there, we go into our mid-week Bible study for an hour. My attendance had been inconsistent. I had been the victim of procrastination. When I heard that the pastor would be teaching on the Holy Ghost, I grew excited. I knew that I would attend the next service.

I arrived late, so I sat on the back row. At the end of the teaching session, Pastor asked us to stand and begin praising God. I remember standing their praising God for how He had changed my attitude toward Holy Ghost night. All I could do was praise Him in my prayer language because of how He had delivered me from all the mental blocks which had kept me from enjoying freedom in the Holy Ghost.

As I was praising God, I felt someone place his hand on my head. When he spoke, I recognized my pastor's voice. He said to me, "Lift your hands and just let Him saturate you." I had been so busy praising God that I did not know that he was even aware of my presence. (He already knew of the many things our family was experiencing because of the mission the Lord had given us.) I yielded to the Holy Ghost as my pastor had directed. I was so glad that I had come to service that night. This was the first time in my life that I could say I loved being in a Holy Ghost night service.

I'm so glad that the God I serve is a deliverer. The Word of God in John's Gospel had been manifested in my life: "If the Son therefore shall make you free, ye shall be free indeed" (John 8:36). I was truly free! I could say that "old things had passed away," and all things had become new (see II Corinthians 5:17).

'Just Do It!'

I remember several years ago I was on my way back to my seat after having received prayer, and one of the missionaries of our church stopped me. The simple words she spoke to me would have a profound effect on my life in ministry.

Before I tell you what she said, I want to tell you what I thought about this lady. She was always the kind of person I wanted to be like. She always seemed to be so in touch with God. She was never fake. She had the kind of relationship with God that I had longed for. She was one beautiful Christian inside and out. (She is now one of the church mothers.) When she spoke in church, whether it was a testimony or a message, I always hung onto her every word.

This is what she said when she stopped me: "Darlene," (I didn't even know she knew my name), "The Lord said, 'Just do it.'" Those were the only words she said. I just shook my head and said, " O.K." For many years, I had seen the saying, "Just do it," on television commercials advertising a famous name brand of shoes and clothing. I had seen it on billboards and practically everywhere I had gone. For several years, the missionary's words echoed in my mind. I kept saying, "Lord, just do what?"

God's timing is not always our timing. Finally, after many years of waiting, the Lord revealed to me the meaning. The Lord said, **"Just do whatever I tell you to do."** The answer seemed so simple that I don't know why it had taken me so long to find the answer. But now I know I have finally come into my season, and the Lord is revealing Himself mightily in my life. Praise God!

Dangers Seen and Unseen

One day I was keeping my great-niece Cortney for Tammy. She is good company for my grandson Jeffrey, whom I baby-sit everyday when school is out. Cortney and Jeffrey had been in the backyard playing when they came running inside to tell me what had just happened. They had seen a man running through our back yard where they were playing, and another man was chasing him on foot. My grandson said the man who was fleeing came so close to him that he had to jump out of his way to keep from being run over. All I could say was, "Thank you Lord for how you watch over our children to protect them."

That afternoon Cortney, Jeffrey and I went on an errand which took us about twenty miles away. As we were returning home on the highway, suddenly cars traveling over sixty-five miles per hour were forced to come to almost a complete stop. There was a stalled car ahead. The truck in front of my car crossed over to the right lane but immediately pulled right back in front of me. No sooner had the truck driver pulled back into my lane, another truck came whizzing by, barely missing the first truck. The car behind me swerved to the left shoulder to keep from hitting me because I had to put on brakes abruptly to keep from hitting the truck ahead of me. I cried, "Oh, Lord, that could have been a terrible accident!"

As soon as the children and I pulled into my driveway way, we saw Tammy coming down the street and she pulled into the driveway behind me. When she came inside, she told me that she had decided to take Cortney to the doctor for a check-up (at the time Cortney was having a problem with a urinary-track infection). While we were talking, I told her we were almost in a wreck on the highway. I was about to ask her if she had seen the stalled car and the police car behind it on the shoulder of the ramp we had been on. While I was asking her if she had seen the car, she kept saying *truck*. As the conversation continued, I discovered that Tammy had been just a few cars behind me, and she had seen the whole thing. Tammy said that she had been saying to herself while the events were unfolding, "Someone up there must be saved because God surely had His hand on that car." When we found out the car she had observed—the one that could have been crushed in an accident—had been my car, we just began to give God the praise for protecting us!

Before Tammy left my house to take Cortney to the doctor, we prayed for Cortney's healing, knowing that by His stripes we are healed. We thanked God right then for her healing by faith in His Word.

The Scottsdale Storm

On July 13, 2001, my husband, grandson and I flew to Scottsdale, Arizona, for a week of vacation in a time-share condominium that we own. I am not sure what day of the week it was, but we had driven to Phoenix to visit our relatives, and for the first time I can remember, we lost our way. Unlike myself, my husband is not one to get lost easily. If he can make it to a place, he can always get back home, even if we are in unfamiliar territory. As much as we have traveled, I cannot remember one instance when my husband was actually lost until that day.

On that particular day, as we were returning to the condo, my husband took a wrong turn. He was aware that he had missed the turn we should have taken, but he kept going, thinking he could take a different turn and get us back to where we were staying. Off in the distance, I could see what appeared to be a white cloud coming down from the sky to the ground, much like when you are riding on a stretch of highway and you can see rain coming down miles away from where you are. What I actually saw was a white cloud stretching from the sky to the ground with a brilliant rainbow forming an arch through the cloud. Actually, the scene was quite beautiful; I had never seen anything like it before. I directed my husband and grandson's attention to the cloud with the rainbow. Although the cloud was white, it appeared to be rain, but where we were, the sun was shining.

My husband saw a man jogging down the street and pulled over to ask him for directions back to Scottsdale. That was the first time I knew that we were lost. The man gave us directions as best he could and wished us good luck.

A short time later, my husband pulled over to a woman getting out of her car and asked her how to get to Scottsdale. He must not have trusted her directions. Finally my husband said, "I'll go back to where I made the wrong turn, and I will get us back to the condo." The entire time my husband was lost, I had been so fascinated by this white cloud with the rainbow running through the middle of it that I had not suspected that anything was wrong. As always, I had no doubt that my husband would find his way back. I was a little amused, however, that he had been so cool and calm during the whole ordeal, and had not even admitted to me that we were lost.

We eventually found the road that led to Scottsdale. As we drew closer to Scottsdale, we could see the white cloud had moved behind Camelback Mountain. The resort where we were staying was situated in front of Camelback Mountain. During the time we were lost, we had not been able to see the mountain at all. Driving into Scottsdale, we saw water and debris in the streets. Several trees lay on the ground. We could tell a terrible storm had hit Scottsdale.

When we arrived at the resort, we were not prepared for what we saw. The entire resort was in disarray—bark from the palm trees lying in the street, no lights on in the office of the resort, bushes lying on the ground. When we entered our unit, the electricity was out, but it came back on just a few minutes later. For several hours, however, the electricity was on and off.

I wanted to share this story because I believe that there was a reason why my husband took a wrong turn and became lost. Ordinarily, we experience a sense of frustration when we lose our way because we fail to reach our destination as planned. However, our getting lost worked in our favor this time. Our Father in heaven kept us from that storm. Not even as much as a drop of rain touched our car. We never felt the violent winds that had swept through that community. Later as we watched the news, we heard that a man had been killed

in the storm. It could have so easily been us—but for
God.

Thank God for Bringing Us Together

I have begun several times to bring my section of
this book to a conclusion. Yes, we have experienced
many miracles, healings, and great blessings from our
God, but we are continuing to seek God's direction in
our lives. We yet have petitions before him regarding
our families.

If you will recall, in Tiffani's vision we were to
pray for the men in our family also. I mentioned earlier
that we all knew we were entering into warfare with
Satan and his armies. Now I believe the level of warfare
has become even greater. It seems as though so many
negative things are happening to the young men, as well
as the older men, in our family. Sometimes it even
seems as though the more we pray, the more life for
them takes a turn for the worse. The saying, "The
darkest hour is just before dawn," certainly seems to
apply to us. But we are comforted by the verse in the
Bible which says, ". . . weeping may endure for a night,
but joy cometh in the morning" (Ps. 30:5). Even the six
of us are finding it hard to attend our prayer circle at the
same time. Because life is pulling us in so many
directions with our children, grandchildren, husbands
and jobs, lately, we just thank God for the times when
all six of us can assemble together. We have never
stopped our circle of prayer, however.

Even though we see problem after problem
cropping up in our families, we still know who has the
victory. We do! We know that in all things, "we are

more than conquerors through him that loved us" (Rom. 8:37). When we listen to the news and hear of so many being killed in the streets, children being abducted and killed, war and terrorism everywhere; we know just how blessed we are! We know that our Father is yet keeping watch over us. Some of our children are out in the streets and many times we do not know where they are, but God, through his Word, makes these promises to those who believe:

- *Thou wilt keep him in perfect peace, whose mind is stayed on thee; because he trusted thee. . .* (Is. 26:3).
- *No weapon that is formed against thee shall prosper. . ."* (Is. 54:17a).
- *". . .great will be the peace of your children* (Is. 54:13b)
- *"For he shall give his angels charge over thee, to keep thee in all thy ways"* (Ps. 91:1).

God's promises of protection are too numerous to mention all of them here. Even though problems come, we have the assurance that God cares for us. Faith in His Word is what keeps us going forward—in spite of the circumstances.

Through the difficult circumstances we are facing, God is drawing each of us closer to Him. I have never in my life enjoyed such a close relationship with God as I do now. It is difficult to explain such a spiritual experience. The best way I can think of to explain my relationship with my heavenly Father is to share with you the difference that being baptized in the

Holy Spirit means. What joy I feel when I come into His presence with praise and thanksgiving! For one thing, I speak in tongues everyday now as the Spirit gives me utterance. I start thinking about how the Lord keeps our families and begin to speak in other tongues. I think of what an awesome God He is and begin to speak in tongues. I can listen to a testimony from someone else and begin speaking in tongues. I know that speaking in tongues isn't everything, but Satan held me captive in a spiritual wilderness for so long because I didn't speak in tongues, that this is something I never dreamed would happen to me. And I love every minute of it!

Somehow, speaking in other tongues, especially when I receive bad news, lets me know that God is going to fix the problem. Therefore, I begin to praise Him more and more as I speak to God in my heavenly language. I love the Lord so much more now than I ever have before, and I know that every single prayer we (the six of us) have prayed, God is going to answer them. Praise our God!

I believe in my heart that if God had not called us to prayer, many in my family, including myself, would not be here today. I am so grateful to the Lord for bringing us together in prayer. No matter the circumstances we face, we are comforted by the words of God spoken by the apostle Paul in the eighth chapter of Romans:

- *For I reckon that the sufferings of this present time are not worthy to be compared with the glory which shall be revealed in us"* (Rom. 8:18), and

- *. . .we know that all things work together for good to them that love God, to them who are the called according to his purpose* (Rom. 8:28).

We know beyond a shadow of doubt that we have been called to His purpose—to serve as intercessors for our family, ever looking to Jesus, the author and finisher of our faith.

By His Power

Our book had already gone to the publisher and was in the final editing phase when we were made aware of what had happened to the drug dealer we had prayed for. We were so blessed by this good news that we thought we would add this testimony to our book. We hope that this testimony of deliverance will bless our readers, too. We give praise and honor to God for what He has done through this prayer ministry. May you be encouraged never to give up on your loved ones whom the devil has taken deeply into drug activity or any other type of sin.

Earlier in this book we talked about a drug house and a drug dealer who lived in our neighborhood. You may remember that he had been in and out of jail for drug-related offenses. In addition to his drug business in our neighborhood, he also frequented the area where our prayer circle converged to engage in spiritual warfare against the negative spirits destroyinging the life of the community. About two weeks after we had submitted our manuscript to the publisher, we talked with the drug dealer's mother, who knew about our weekly prayer.

She was so excited as she listened to her son telling what the Lord had done for him.

The dealer had left town to enter drug rehabilitation. (We had missed seeing him, but we did not know his whereabouts.) When he returned, he was a different person. It was wonderful listening to the now *former* drug dealer quote Scripture and share about the power of God through prayer. He confessed to me that he realized God had been with him the entire time he was in the world doing his own thing. He also said he knew that he had been called to be a preacher. He has now committed his life to the Lord.

Lord, we thank You with all of our hearts for being God Almighty, and for doing just what You said You would do in II Chronicles 7:14, "If my people, which are called by my name, shall humble themselves, and pray, and seek my face, and turn from their wicked ways; then will I hear from heaven, and will forgive their sin, and will heal their land."

Section II

Sharon's
TESTIMONIES

Father, fill me with Your wisdom,
and let the light of Your Son
shine through me....

Getting To Know Me

I know now that, because of the prayers of my mother and grandparents, God's hand has always been on my life. As a child I remember their praying for me through the night when I had trouble breathing because of asthma. When I was a teenager the school nurse would send me home because I suffered cramps so badly. My mother was at work, so I would take a cab to my grandmother's house. I experienced firsthand the power of prayer. I remember my grandmother placing her hand on my stomach and praying, and the pain would go away.

When I was a teenager, Mama would let me go out on dates. Coming into the house, I would pass her bedroom door before I reached my room, and I would see Mama on her knees in prayer. Mama did a lot of praying, and now I understand why. She was raising six children, four boys and two girls, with an alcoholic husband. Mama had been saved since she was twelve years old. She was a beautiful, sweet, soft-spoken woman, but we knew to move when she spoke. We never heard her raise her voice—never heard a curse word come from her mouth. Even as children, we could see the power of God in her life.

My dad's parents were always close to us and gave my mother any natural and spiritual support she needed. We were never short on food, clothes, or shoes; if we were poor, we certainly did not know it. We always had everything we needed. God blessed us through our grandparents, who were saved and shared not only with us but with other people in the neighborhood and church as well.

Our grandparents, whom we called "Gram" and "Gramps," were an integral part of our lives. Just knowing that they loved us made all the difference in the world. Once my fourth-grade teacher asked me how I kept my socks so white. I owed my white socks to my grandmother. She lived next door to us and did all our washing. She soaked and bleached our socks, and they were always white. She was always doing things for us. Gram often canned vegetables from the huge garden that my grandfather grew (which not only fed us, but the neighbors also). The luscious fruit from the fruit trees, grapevines, and strawberry patch, she turned into delicious jams and jellies. Gramps would give me a nickel to pick strawberries from the strawberry patch. (Of course, all the strawberries didn't go into the basket.) They demonstrated their love for us in so many ways. Just knowing that they loved God and seeing how they lived a life that "walked the walk and talked the talk" of their faith gave us a stability and a foundation that we may not have otherwise known.

When I was ten or eleven years old, I used to curse because my best friend did, and I wanted to be like her. Of course, my family did not know it. Then in the spring of the year that I turned thirteen, I was saved in a revival. I felt great. I felt the Spirit of the Lord in me, and it was wonderful. (You know how you felt when you were first saved.) That Monday when I went back to school, I slipped and said a curse word, and immediately that great feeling left. At the time I did not understand that my salvation was not so fragile. I did not know that all I had to do was sincerely repent of my wrongdoing, and my Father would, by His grace, forgive me and receive me back into His arms.

As a teenager I struggled with living a saved life. I seemed to always be on a roller coaster in my spiritual life—up and down, in and out of church. Because I was not truly grounded in the Lord, I was not prepared to handle the disappointments that came my way. My grandmother passed when I was twenty-four years old, and my mother passed when I was twenty-seven. By the time I was thirty, I was doing things that, when I look back, I know I would never have done if they had still been alive.

I no longer cared about living saved. I felt that God had taken away too soon two beautiful people that meant the world to me. I had been married to a husband who had been unfaithful during the entire course of our marriage (which lasted fourteen years before I divorced him), and I felt that I was raising our two daughters by myself. During that time, although my mother and grandmother were gone, I knew that it had been their prayers that kept me from harm. I was not praying for myself, but God was still protecting my girls and me.

At this time in my life I made some really bad choices. Although I was pregnant when we married, I had never been with anyone else but my husband. We had been married about ten years when I discovered that my husband had been cheating during our entire marriage. (I actually knew of one indiscretion after we had been married five years, but silly me, I thought that this had been an isolated incident.) Many of my family had known about my husband's infidelity, but no one told me until then. Realizing that my husband had never been true to me, coupled with the death of my wonderful grandmother and then my mother, I turned away from God. I justified my actions by saying I had the right to live my life the way I pleased, thinking I was hurting no one but myself. I could not see the true consequences. Satan has a way of blinding us to the truth. You do not realize at the time that those indiscretions can follow you forever.

When I discovered for the first time (about five years into our marriage) that my husband had been unfaithful to our marriage vows, I was wiped out emotionally. It was as if someone close to me had died. First, I had difficulty believing it; then I became angry, and I wanted to hurt him. Somewhere in my mind I thought I was not pretty enough, not intelligent enough for him, or I did not satisfy him sexually. Eventually, I stopped blaming myself for his infidelity. I told myself it did not matter what he had done, I had my girls and I would build my life around them. I thought I was able to tolerate his behavior. After suffering five more years of infidelity, I discovered that my children did not seem to provide the fulfillment that I needed, and I started looking for happiness outside of my marriage.

There I was, looking for love in all the wrong places, trying to find someone who would really love me. It seems that that detour of about three or four years of my life will haunt me the rest of my life. My mother would always tell me, "You do what you know is right and when you look back, you will not have any regrets." I wish I had remembered her words of wisdom while I was on my quest for 'happiness.' I would tell anyone who is hurting because of a painful relationship, and is looking for revenge, that revenge is not so sweet. Revenge is never the answer. Christ is the only answer

—always. Seeking revenge only brings more pain and heartache.

That one interlude in my life has caused me so much pain. Well over twenty years have passed, and I know that I repented long ago and God has surely forgiven me, but I still find that I go through the process of forgiving myself over and over. I know that God does not remember our sins once we have received forgiveness, but Satan keeps throwing my past in my face. After all, I furnished him the ammunition. I rebuke Satan and go on with my life. I cannot erase those years, although I desperately wish I could, but I do pray that young people will not make the same mistakes I made. When the attacks of Satan come against you, and you feel like quitting or you begin to contemplate ungodly actions, just remember that there is no safer place in the universe than in your walk with Jesus Christ.

I returned to the Lord and recommitted my life to Him when I was in my middle thirties. My girls were teenagers then, and I needed to be in a position where I could pray, not only for myself, but for them also. In the beginning turning away from all the things of the world was a tremendous struggle. I thank God for my pastor's wife, a Spirit-filled lady who counseled me and labored with me during that time, admonishing me and helping me to make the right decisions. She invited me to dinner and spent all evening encouraging me to do the right thing because she knew some of the issues I was facing. We sat and talked at the restaurant until closing time. I will always be grateful for the time she took helping me establish my steps as I recommitted my life to Christ.

I lost friends and relationships, but God filled me with His Holy Spirit, which gave me the power to resist the things that would have drawn me away from Him. I belong to a Bible-believing church whose leaders are Spirit-filled and they preach the Word of God. They not only preach the Word, but they live by it also. We have wonderful prayer meetings and Bible study sessions, and my faith and understanding in the Lord has matured.

At the age of thirty-eight, God blessed me with a saved husband who wanted only me, and believe me, after my first husband, that was a big thing. The first few years were a challenge, but God has blessed us with a loving marriage. We attend church together, we serve in church together, and we love being together and doing things together. I thank God for him daily. We are in a place in our lives now where we are enjoying the blessings of God. Our children are grown and have come home for the last time (we hope). We have wonderful grandchildren, and God continues to bless us.

Attacks on My Physical Body

As an adult, I have generally enjoyed reasonably good health, even though I have been overweight most of my life. Aside from having gallstones removed when I was twenty years old, and suffering minor sinus and allergy problems in my adult years, I have not known much sickness. This came to a halt a few years ago when I was very sick for a few days with what appeared to be influenza. Because I did not know if I had the flu, or maybe food poisoning, I went to the emergency room.

Since I had suffered the flu maybe twice in my fifty plus years, I was not certain what was wrong with me, but I surely wanted to know.

The medical staff completed routine medical procedures. The blood work revealed that my blood sugar level was extremely high, so the technician poked me again to recheck it. Eventually, the doctor on duty treated me for the flu and sent me home. The results of my tests would be sent to my doctor (one I had not seen before, but I had an appointment with her in two weeks).

When the doctor's office received the results of the test, I received a call from her nurse, who advised me to come to her office as soon as possible. When I arrived, the doctor told me the same thing that the doctor had told me in the emergency room—my sugar level was high, but she wanted to recheck it to confirm the results. Upon taking another blood sample, the doctor informed me that the results were the same—my blood sugar reading was abnormal, and she diagnosed me as having Type II diabetes. I tried to talk to the doctor on a faith level and let her know that I expected to be healed, but she did not want to hear that. She was very adamant about my being on medication and, of course, watching what I ate and getting plenty of exercise. I did as my doctor advised and claimed my healing anyway. My expectations of being healed were kept between my family and friends and my prayer partners and me.

I was put on medication right away and an appointment was made for me to see a nutritionist to learn how to prepare my meals, and receive a meter so I could monitor my blood sugar two to three times a day. I kept my appointment with the nutritionist, at which time she took me through some *do's* and *don'ts* of my diet and proceeded to demonstrate the meter. She pricked my finger to test my sugar level. My blood sugar count was so high that it went off the meter, and the meter sounded an alarm. The nutritionist called my doctor's office immediately. The doctor said she would call in a prescription for insulin to the pharmacy and that I should pick up the insulin and bring it to her office after work, at which time she would show me how to give myself shots.

I tried not to show it, but I was struck with terror. I went to work and planned to follow my doctor's instructions, to pick up the insulin and go to her office after work. As soon as I arrived at my office, I called my husband to let him know what had happened. I do not know what he was really thinking, but he encouraged me as he always does. Then I called my daughter Tiffani and, not wanting to upset her or let her know the panic I was feeling, I calmly told her the events of the morning and had her call her sister, Tammy, and her Aunt Darlene, because I could not keep repeating the entire story. I kept telling myself, "You can handle this; you can handle this." My family immediately began to pray for me.

Upon arrival at the doctor's office that afternoon, the technician drew my blood again. My blood sugar level was low enough that the doctor did not think I needed the insulin. I was rejoicing in my heart and praising the Lord. She did tell me, however, to keep the medicine on the shelf for the future. (I eventually threw the medication away, after the expiration date; I never had to use it.) Later when I told my family the *good news,* that I did not need insulin, my daughter said, "Mama, when I got off the phone with you I went on my face in prayer." Tears came to my eyes, and they still do, when I think of the awesomeness of God and how He put praying people in my life. With everything that had happened that morning I was so upset that I did not think to pray for myself. Thank God for my prayer partners.

I started two different medications and monitored my blood sugar levels twice a day. I walked on the treadmill daily and was very conscience of what I ate. It helped immensely that I was participating in the *Daniel Fast* that the pastor had called for the congregation. During this fast we eliminated sweets, caffeine, pop, and red meats from our diets, and the only television programs we watched were Christian TV and the news. (This is one of the fasts that my pastor calls periodically to help the congregation draw in to a closer relationship with the Lord.) This was just what I needed to help me develop discipline in my diet.

Initially, my doctor visits were scheduled every two weeks so that the doctor could closely monitor my progress. I was doing so well keeping my blood sugar levels down and steadily loosing weight that I was taken off one of the medications. In the meantime, my prayer partners and I were praying for my complete healing. After about two months of going through the same process, my sugar levels stayed in normal range. When I checked it in the morning, it was normal, so I stopped taking my medicine and called the doctor. I did not want my sugar level to drop too low. The doctor agreed and took me off that medication.

I have since changed my eating habits. I don't get enough exercise, but that has to change too. I thank God that I don't have to take pills the rest of my life for sugar diabetes. I thank Him for healing me. I appreciate the wisdom of a great television evangelist who said in one of his messages, "Claim your healing and eat right." Those were truly words to *live* by.

Hurdling Another Challenge

I was so glad God had blessed me with such good doctors. They were definitely a godsend at that time in my life. I had changed doctors because I did not think my previous doctor had been proactive enough in trying to prevent illnesses and diseases. My new doctors ordered various kinds of tests, one of which was a colonoscopy, partly because of my age and also because of my family medical history. (My mother had died of colon cancer; an aunt and first cousin also had died at a young age of different types of cancer. My aunt was thirty-two years old and my first cousin, forty-three).

I was just a little girl when my mother's youngest sister passed away, and from that point on, I thought somehow that I would not live past the age of thirty-two. Although I did not die at that age, I knew I would not live past forty-three. Well, I made it. By the time I was approaching the age at which my mother died, my prayer partners and I had already prayed that the curse of cancer and all diseases be broken off our family. I was no longer bound by the fear that had previously haunted me. I knew the curse had been broken. I believed that, not only for myself, but also for my children and my children's children.

The test I had taken revealed two polyps. One was small enough for the doctor to remove at the time of the test, but the other one required surgery. The thought of surgery was extremely troubling and I stalled awhile before I finally set a date.

I did not intend to share my problems with anyone else outside my family, but as I made arrangements for things to be attended to in my absence, (being in ministry in my church) I found it necessary to confide in a few people. Every person with whom I shared stopped immediately to pray for me. Even the girl whom I had just met, as she braided my hair in preparation for the surgery, prayed for my recovery. One lady even told me she would pray that I had no pain after my surgery. She had recently had surgery on her shoulder, and that prayer had been prayed for her, and she experienced no pain after the surgery. When the lady said that to me, my first reaction was one of disbelief. How could I have major surgery and have no pain? I had undergone major surgery years before, and I still remembered feeling so terrible that I thought I would never be well again. I dismissed doubt, and by faith, quickly grabbed hold to what she was saying. After all, what did I have to lose except a lot of pain?

I had been covered by so much prayer that my surgery went well. It could not have been any other way. When I awoke the first day I was hooked up to a machine that automatically dispensed pain medication, but I was experiencing only minor pain. After that first day I needed no more pain medication. When the pathology report came back, I had another reason to rejoice. The polyp was benign! The surgeon told me that if the polyp had remained there six more months, it would have developed into cancer. He seemed delighted at how well I had healed and was very pleased at his handy work. My heart rejoiced at the cancer-free report, even though I had not expected the surgeon to find cancer because of the prayers of our group and everyone else who had prayed for me. Indeed, the 'curse of cancer' had been broken off our family. That is an issue that we had addressed in many of our weekly prayers. And I believe it! (A year later was my next scheduled colonoscopy and, praise God, the report was good!)

Faith Transferred

I know in my heart that my sister, Darlene, has joined that great cloud of witnesses mentioned by Paul in Hebrews chapter eleven. Their testimonies assure us of what can be accomplished through faith. God prepared me for what was in store for me by letting me witness the faith He had given my sister. If I had not seen her go through her illness with such conviction, standing on the Word, "by His stripes I am healed," (and she never wavered) I may have lacked the courage to face my test. She has the 'gift of faith,' a standing in God which took her through day after day, and through radiation treatment after radiation treatment. This was the faith she shared with me and put in my heart and mind.

I began to see through her eyes of faith. She had this faith for me, and I could not let her down. I knew what God's Word had to say about divine healing. I had read it for myself many times. It was in my head, but God made it more real than ever to me through what Darlene had experienced, and she poured her faith into my life. She constantly recited Isaiah 53: 5, "But He was wounded for our transgressions, he was bruised for our iniquities: the chastisement of our peace was upon him; and with his *stri*pes we are healed." That verse became the battle cry that resonated in our hearts and souls for any physical affliction the enemy hurled at us.

Selling Our House

My husband and I had periodically, over a couple of years, talked about selling our house. We wanted to sell at the most opportune time, before our neighborhood began to decline, in order to reap the most from our investment. We really liked our house and the neighborhood, so it was easy to put off making a move. We would watch the interest rates change, yet we did not make a move. It seemed as though we had always been slow about making financial decisions. How long should we keep our car before trading it in? Should or should we not sell our two rental houses? Of course, the missing factor was consulting with the Lord about what steps to take.

My younger daughter, Tiffani, had moved out of the county and started encouraging us to do the same, citing that where she lived was a better area. It was quiet, had less crime and lower taxes. She shared how she had made her transition. When she had made her move, she asked the Lord to let her house sell in so many days after she had put it on the market; she also told the Lord how much she wanted for her house. The Lord had answered her prayers, and I knew he would answer mine also, because he is not a respecter of persons (see Acts 10:34).

When we decided to put our house on the market, we asked the Lord to let it sell quickly. At prayer I asked my prayer partners to pray for our success in selling our home. Tiffani told me to be more specific, so we asked that our home sell within a month. I also did not want to have to move more than once, so we asked that we find a house that we could afford in a timely manner. Another problem was trying to decide what price to put on our house. The amount that I came up with was $30,000 more than what we had paid for it, and that was a stretch, in my estimation, but my husband and daughter thought that the price I had suggested was not enough. We added an additional $25,000 and later found out that the house had actually been appraised for more than the figure we recommended. We put the house on the market and we had a buyer in two weeks. Of course, we were required to make repairs, but the Lord blessed us to meet our obligations. We put in a new furnace, had the roof repaired, and completed some additional carpentry work—all without having to make a bill doing any of it. We had never seemed to have any extra money before, so it was amazing that we could do this without getting a loan.

We began making preparations to purchase our new home. When we applied for a mortgage loan, we were pre-approved for an amount that baffled me. I could not understand why we had been approved for so much. What kind of figures were those folks looking at? The buyers wanted to take possession of our home by the end of the month. At that point we had not found a house to move to, so we asked for thirty additional days. Fortunately for us, we had already been searching for a new home for a couple of months, and had narrowed our search to the northland area where Tiffani lived (what a surprise!). The Sunday after the contract was put on our house, we had an appointment to look at another house—one that we had passed by before because, from the outside it appeared to be a two-story, and we were looking for a ranch style. To our surprise, when we went inside, we discovered that everything was on one level. We knew that this house was 'the one.'

The first of December, 2000—a day I will always remember—we signed the papers to close on the selling our house that morning, and that afternoon we closed on the house we were purchasing. In doing so, another prayer had been answered: We did not have to move twice. We moved right from our old house to our new house in one day. We had been in our other house for less than fourteen years, and we almost doubled our investment. We had prayed that the house would sell in a month, and it sold in two weeks. We had enough money to put twenty percent down on our new house, and enough money left over to pay off several bills. Also, we were able to buy large appliances and furnishings, and there was still money left to finish the lower level, which immediately increased our property value by $20,000.

Nine months after we had moved into our new home, we witnessed one of the greatest acts of terrorism this country has ever known. At the end of September of 2001, because of the economy, the events of September 11 (9/11), and our company's downsizing, I was laid off a job that I had held for nineteen years. But because God is so good, He had put us in a new house with most of our bills paid off, and had blessed me with an earlier retirement than I had expected (which means a check comes every month). My husband would be able to handle the rest of the bills. God is faithful to His promises.

Through the years my husband and I have always been tithers, and we stand on the Word of God and His promises as stated in Malachi 3:10–11: "Bring ye all the tithes into the storehouse, that there may be meat in mine house, and prove me now herewith, saith the Lord of hosts, if I will not open you the windows of heaven, and pour you out a blessing, that there shall not be room enough to receive it." We count on God to do just what His Word says—to pour out His blessings upon all of us.

From time to time, I walk through my new home, thanking the Lord for this blessing. Sometimes I wonder to myself how this could have happened. How did we get here? We have been here almost two years and, I am still amazed at how God has blessed us. I know that many people have much more than we do, but this does not diminish the greatness of God in our lives. He has shared with us of His abundance, according to Ephesians 4:20–21, "Now unto him that is able to do exceeding abundantly above all that we ask or think, according to the power that worketh in us, Unto him be glory in the church by Christ Jesus throughout all ages, world without end. Amen." We give God the glory. He certainly did more for us than we ever expected, or even hoped for. This experience taught me never to limit God. He wants to give us His best, and, of course, He had already given us his best—His only begotten son, Jesus Christ.

Prayer for Our Aunt

On some prayer nights we would venture out to pray for family and friends in hospitals and in their homes. Occasionally, we would have someone visit our group and pray with us. One week during our prayer time we went to our aunt's house because she was scheduled for major surgery the next morning. Contemplating her surgery, she was somewhat nervous and fretful. She had recently lost her husband and companion of more than forty years (our uncle), and she was alone and afraid as she faced open-heart surgery.

When we arrived at her house, we could see she was visibly shaken, and all we wanted to do was to comfort her. We wanted to let her know that we were praying for her because God is faithful, and He is a healer. We prayed that she would have peace of mind. We also prayed for a successful surgery, and because God had blessed me to have very little pain, and then no pain; we prayed that she would experience no pain, and that she would have a quick recovery.

When our prayer group went to visit our aunt in the hospital, she was doing well. The operation had been successful. In spite of having undergone open-heart surgery, she was not in pain. Her recovery was quick, and she was soon dismissed from the hospital, but the doctor prescribed temporary use of oxygen at home. After a few months of recovery, our aunt moved back to her hometown in Texas. She was buying a house there and was enjoying being reunited with her siblings and other family members.

We were surprised later when we received a call from a relative in Texas, telling us our aunt had been admitted to the hospital. The doctor had discovered a huge mass (tumor), which he later reported to be cancerous. He did not know how far the cancer had spread in her body. We were told that he would operate immediately. Some of us thought that since our aunt was up in age that this was probably 'it' for her. We had almost given up until we talked to Darlene, the one with supernatural faith. She said, "Not so!" She reminded us that we had prayed to break the curse of cancer, and we were not letting Satan make us take a step backward. We began to pray and intercede for our aunt. We reminded God that we had prayed for the curse of cancer to be broken off our family, and we believed that it was done.

We, the prayer group, knew we needed to travel to Texas to be with our aunt for surgery, but Darlene's purpose was deeper than that. She said that it was not enough just to be there by our aunt's bedside, but we needed to go and lay hands on our aunt and pray for her recovery, according to the Scriptures: "A*nd these signs shall follow them that believe; in My name shall they cast out devils; they shall speak with new tongues; They shall take up serpents; and if they drink any deadly thing, it shall not hurt them; they shall lay hands on the sick, and they shall recover" (Mark 16:17, 18).* This we did, for we believed in God's Word.

Two other members of our prayer circle accompanied me to Texas—Darlene and Mashan. We went prepared to battle. (our oldest brother and his wife met us there.) When we arrived, our cousin and her daughter were there by our aunt's side, taking care of her needs. They were there for the long haul, staying for weeks to help our aunt take care of her business. They would be there for her to lean on.

Our aunt's surgery had been delayed for a few days because her oxygen level was low. The doctor was also concerned about her emphysema. We were not able to stay until she had surgery, but we prayed for her a few times while we were there. After we arrived home we received the good news; the surgery had been successful, and there was **no cancer**. The doctor was baffled. He said he knew what he had seen, and he knew that my aunt had been full of cancer. The fact remained, however, that when the surgery was done, the doctor found no cancer. We thank God for proving Himself to us over and over again.

The last word we heard about our aunt was that she was doing well in Texas, and had called relatives in the Midwest, requesting that her evening gowns be shipped to her.

Taking Prayer to the Streets

One Thursday evening as we were concluding our weekly prayer, Tiffani began to pray for the community. Nearing the end of our prayer, our eyes still closed, we meditated on the goodness of the Lord. I could see our prayer group standing on a corner praying. I recognized the location immediately. I had grown up in that neighborhood, and I drive pass that corner often. Drug dealers and prostitutes saturate the area. I saw us there, but I did not want to say anything to the group about what I was seeing. I sat there quietly as the rest fellowshipped as we usually do—just girl talk. I finally found the courage to speak.

"I had a vision of us standing on the corner of Thirty-first and Brown praying for the community," I said. Then I added quickly, "You know we have to do this. The Lord doesn't show me too many visions, but He showed me that one."

A week or so had passed when Darlene reminded me of the vision during a telephone conversation. "You know we have to go up on Brown and pray," she said. All I could say was, "I know." Later we agreed on a date and decided to go early on a Saturday morning, while the drug dealers, addicts, and prostitutes were still asleep. I must admit that I was feeling somewhat intimidated.

Monday of the week we were to pray, the Lord woke me up early with a message of what we were to do during our prayer. Wanting to make sure we did not forget exactly what we needed to pray for, I began to write what the Lord was telling me. The Lord gave me scriptures of encouragement and faith. He assured me that He would give us the boldness to accomplish what He had shown me. We began three days of fasting and praying on Wednesday in preparation for our appointment on Saturday. We did not want to be like the disciples who were ignored by the demons when they were trying to cast the demons out because the disciples had not fasted and prayed. In other words, they had not prepared themselves for the battle. We would follow God's plan, and we knew He would be with us. What God sends you to do, He will equip you to do. The text of the prayer that God wanted us to pray at the corner of Thirty-first and Brown is listed on the next page.

Prayer for Thirty-first and Brown

For God so loved the world that He gave His only begotten son, that whosoever believeth in Him should not perish, but have everlasting life (John 3:16). Thank You, Lord, for placing in our hearts the need to go to Thirty-first and Brown to pray for the people and this community. Thank You because You let us know that all we had to do was **say** it, and You would take care of everything else.

Thank You for giving us the boldness to go to that corner to rebuke devils, because we know that You are with us, for Your Word says: *"For where two or three are gathered together in my name, there am I in the midst of them"* (Matt. 18:20).

We thank You because II Tim.1:7 says, *"For God hath not given us a spirit of fear; but of power and love, and of a sound mind."*

Thank You, Lord, *because "There shall no evil befall thee, neither shall any plague come nigh thy dwelling. For he shall give his angels charge over thee, to keep thee in all thy ways"* (Ps. 91:10,11).

"For whom he did foreknow, he also did predestinate to be conformed to the image of his Son, that he might be the firstborn among many brethren. . . What shall we then say to these things? If God be for us, who can be against us" (Rom. 8:29,31)?

"Peace I leave with you, my peace I give unto you: not as the world giveth, give I unto you. Let not your heart be troubled, neither let it be afraid" (John 14:27).

We thank You, Lord, because we know that You hear us and **You will** answer our prayers.

Thank You, Lord, for preparing us and strengthening us through Your Word. Thank You for encouraging us through times of consecration—prayer and fasting—because this is what is needed to defeat the enemy and put him to flight. Thank You, Lord, for giving us the courage to step out and do what You showed us we needed to do.

And now, Lord, we stand before Your throne of grace on behalf of our brethren. We know it is not Your will that any should perish. Lord, it is Your will that we are here this moment, at this time, to stand in the gap for those who have been deceived by the enemy. We are gathered here in Your Name and we know that You are here with us.

Lord, we pray not only for the people that populate and inhabit this corner, but we pray for the entire community. Father, take the spiritual blinders off so they can see the destruction which will befall them in the future, unless they accept Your Son Jesus Christ into their lives as their personal Savior. Lord, deliver them from the enemy.

And right now, Lord, we take authority over Satan and all his demons and powers, and we come against him in the Name of Jesus Christ to cast out the devils that plague the people and this area. We take the authority that You won back for us at Calvary. We plead the blood of Jesus over this area and us all and ask that you make this area whole again—in the Name of Jesus. We stand on the promise you made to Peter in Your Word:

> *And I say unto thee, that thou art Peter,*
> *and upon this rock I will build my church; and*
> *the gates of hell will not prevail against it. And I*

will give unto thee the keys of the kingdom of heaven: and whatsoever thou shalt bind on earth shall be bound in heaven: and whatsoever thou shalt loose on earth shall be loosed in heaven (Matt. 16:18,19).

Now, Father, in Jesus' Name, we cast out the demons of. . . .

- drug addiction
- hopelessness
- alcohol addiction
- condemnation
- idolatry
- fornication, adultery
- poverty
- unforgiveness (self and others)
- lust
- pride
- murder
- feeling unloved/unwanted
- anger
- suicide
- prostitution
- low self-esteem
- deceit
- rebellion
- disease/sickness (mind, body, spirit)
- hatred
- laziness
- ungratefulness
- conceit
- fear

- depression
- lack of wisdom

And, Father, in Your Name, we loose the spirits of. . .

- the Love of God
- healing of mind, body, and spirit
- the spirit of fellowship
- the joy and peace of the God
- the spirit of goodwill
- health/wellness
- happiness
- wealth
- humbleness
- a nurturing spirit
- a God-seeking spirit
- a faithful spirit

We are confident in You to hear and answer our prayers:

> *And this is the confidence that we have in Him, if we ask anything according to His will, He heareth us: And if we know that He hear us, whatsoever we ask, we know that we have the petitions that we desire of Him* (I John 5:14, 15).

> *And these signs shall follow them that believe; In My name shall they cast out devils; they shall speak with new tongues* (Mark 16:17).

> *The Lord is not slack concerning his promise, as some men count slackness; but is longsuffering to us-ward, not willing that any*

should perish but that all should come to repentance (II Pet. 3:9).

Lord, we pray for good, honorable policemen that have a heart for the people, who want to help the young people and not hurt them. We pray for good, moral leadership in the local and national governments—leaders who want to help all communities and all people, leaders who will take a stand and protect all the citizen. We pray for leaders who will clean up the neighborhoods and get rid of drug houses and prostitution to make our neighborhoods safe.

And we know that the Son of God is come, and hath given us an understanding, that we may know him that is true, and we are in him that is true, [even] in his Son Jesus Christ. This is the true God, and eternal life (I John 5:20). Amen.

We assembled that rainy Saturday morning in Darlene's driveway and prayed before we drove to Thirty-first and Brown. We stood on the corner in the rain, and as I read the prayer that God had given me, the others prayed in tongues. Afterwards, we stapled four copies of the prayer on the telephone post. One was facing north, one south, one east and one west, symbolizing our prayers going out in all directions. We wanted the people there to know that someone had been praying for them. The prayer copies stayed on the post for several days until they slowly disappeared, one by one.

It is our responsibility as ambassadors of Christ to be kingdom builders. The Lord has given us not only to pray for our families, but also to do spiritual warfare in the heavenly realm for our communities.

How Sweet It Is!

Life is so much sweeter because of my prayer partners. I never have to face any situation alone. I do not have to rely on my faith along. I can make one phone call and have several people going before God on my behalf with me. I may not always know how to present my request to the Lord, I may not have the right words, but someone will know just what to say. We have learned over time how to approach Him and make our request known. We meet and meditate on His goodness before entering into His presence. My husband is very sweet and supportive, and I love him dearly, but there is something a little different when 'the girls' come together. The fellowship and love we feel toward one another is hard to explain.

I cannot thank God enough for binding us together in this way. When I try to remember our relationships before we began praying together, it seems almost as if we have always been together praying. I cannot imagine us ever stopping. God, in His infinite wisdom, brought us together and is blessing us to experience abundant life in Him. Not all our prayers have been answered, but God has blessed us with faith to know that He will answer our prayers. He gives us joy and peace in the midst of our trials. The obstacles I have to face in life, I do so, knowing that my prayer group 'has my back.'

Sometimes When I Pray

When I pray, my prayers are simple. I begin by thanking Him and praising Him for all of His blessings—from the smallest things to those very precious to my heart. From thanksgiving and praise, I then move to the prayer of forgiveness. I ask forgiveness for my sins and shortcomings because I do not want anything standing between God and me. My prayers then flow back into thanksgiving, and continue to move back and forth from thanksgiving to petition.

I thank Him for life and for the healing my body. I thank Him for a saved husband and children and for keeping His arms of protection around us. I ask Him to preserve our lives. I ask Him to pour out His blessings on us and to cover us with His blood. I bless His Holy name and thank Him for His faithfulness. I recite His Words back to Him to receive His bountiful blessings. I stand on His promises shown throughout the Bible as I pray, believing that He hears me and will answer my prayers.

SECTION III

Mashan's TESTIMONIES

Thank You, Lord, for Your trials,
tribulations, and victories....

My Family Prayer Group

This is the testimony of a family whose foundation was built by God through prayer. I can remember my great-grandmother and grandmother singing and praying all the time, and we attended church regularly. The next two generations of women (on my father's side) are saved also, and are continuing the family heritage. Not many people can say that the women through whom their blood runs are indeed saved. This is so awesome to me.

The key to life itself—that is eternal life, planned before the foundation of the world—is prayer. We have seen miracles and destruction during these two years of prayer, but I cannot imagine what our lives would be like if we were not praying for our family.

Together, as an army with a strategic plan, we fight for our family's salvation and protection. The six of us come together once a week for however long the Holy Spirit directs, to pray, and sometimes fast, for our loved ones. I have never met a family quite like ours. We not only love one another, but we also are in love with one another. We are so close spiritually that we can share things and come to a greater understanding spiritually because we are all on one accord. We have bonded in a way that is hard to express, but we do know that we are on a mission to do whatever it takes until everyone in our family is saved.

Believe me when I say this is war, for there are always battles to fight. From the moment this prayer group started, the enemy declared war, and so did we. Though we become weary sometimes, we continue to fight because we have the greatest cause for which to fight—our family. This life is but a test. The next one is forever.

I am Mashan, the daughter of Richard Minor, who was the brother of Sharon and Darlene. I am the cousin of Tammy, Tiffani and Shontelle. Shontelle and I were raised in the same household. She is like a little sister to me.

My Sons: Nicholos, Aaron, and Dajuan

Many of the stories that I am about to share took place over a period of three years during our family prayer; others occurred prior to that time period. In battle after battle, we were challenged in everything that mattered to us, especially our family. There is always a fight in the spirit when *you know that you know that you know* you are doing what God is telling you to do. Romans 8:37 tells us that "we are more than conquerors through Him that loved us." The devil knows this and he goes straight to your heart for the kill, to stop you in your tracks, but we know we are victorious in the end.

Nicholos

I will start with Nick, my oldest son, who is in the United States Navy on the East coast. When he called to let me that he was getting married to someone several years older than he (he was only twenty at the time), I was concerned. I had gone through a 'bad' experience with my son's fiancée on the phone, so I fought the upcoming marriage. My son, proceeded with the his plans, however, in spite of my many objections.

Through wisdom, I have learned to accept my son's marriage. I know that God put her in my life for a purpose, and I know that whatever the reason, it's for my good because I do love God (see Romans 8:28).

My children and I are very close. If I had chosen to reject this marriage, I would have lost my relationship with my son. The devil knows just where and how to hurt us, but God knows how to counter-attack. In short, the enemy thought he would cause division among us; instead, God dealt with me about forgiveness. The Lord told me that He could not use us if we have unforgiveness in our hearts. My daughter-in-law and I are moving toward building a relationship. Now I have two granddaughters whom I adore.

Aaron

My second son, Aaron—the eighteen-year-old college student-football player—is a good son. He is a member of the Army Reserve, and is saved, but he is struggling with some issues. When he went to boot camp, basically, he was made a target. First of all, his recruiting officer sent him to camp with no supplies. Then his comrades said he smiled too much.

While Aaron was at camp, he almost had a break down. He suffered food poisoning and was hospitalized. We prayed and prayed, but the more we prayed, the angrier the devil became. Upset over something that had gone wrong, Aaron would call me, wanting to be released from duty, but there was nothing I could do, physically. But spiritually, our prayer group launched an attack against Satan. First, we came before God with repentance so there would not be anything between God and us.   Repentance was followed by thanksgiving. We gave thanks to God for what He had already ordained. We moved into praise and worship, to magnify and glorify His name.   Our praise and worship shifted to another level, praying in tongues, and we knew He would receive from us what He needed, without the enemy or our knowing exactly what it was that we needed to pray for.

This was one of the best prayer meetings we had ever had, but they kept getting better and stronger. Together, we were bonding more closely. We knew that there was no limit to what we could do in the Name of Jesus (see Philippians 4:13).

Aaron was finally released. from the Army and returned home safely.   The lesson I learned from this experience was to stand on God's Word, no matter how situations look. God is always right on time.

Dajuan

Dajuan, my youngest son, was the dream child. He did not cry, he crawled at three months, and he potty trained himself. He saw his brothers go to the bathroom, and he did the same. I never had to train him. He was quiet, very observant, and loved to be around my brother and my cousin. He loved keys, cars, and cowboy boots. He and his two brothers were five and six years apart. I guess he was the least of my worries at that time.

In his early teens Dajuan started running with the wrong crowd, staying out late, and being disrespectful. I'm from the old school. I do not believe in sparing the rod and spoiling the child. I do believe in using the rod, taking names, and not even thinking about asking questions.

The battle began. At first, Dajuan would run away from home and come back the same day. Then days would go by and I would not see him at all. These were some of the worst times for me. The worst feeling in the world for a mother is not to know where her child is. If you have never experienced it, you do not want to—that sickening feeling in your stomach that causes acid reflux to burn inside you, the despair and hopelessness of living in a neighborhood where killings occur frequently, the heaviness in your chest when the phone rings, sitting in the window for what seems like hours just waiting for your son to walk up on the porch. The numbness in your spirit causes tears to stream down your cheeks. Yet the Lord had said to me, "It's only a test." I thought, "This is going to be a hard one." Enduring the ups and downs of an emotional roller coaster ride, I cried out, "Where is my baby?"

Taking advantage of your emotional state, the devil starts playing a movie in your mind. You see your child's funeral. How long will you let it play before you rebuke him and pray? It is a non-stop battle—one that can wear you out physically and mentally. It's easy for someone to say, "Trust God and pray. It will be all right." You do all these things, but you still don't know where your child is.

Still you sing, "I trust you, Lord." Then you cry out in despair. You fast and pray with others, yet no Dajuan. Phone calls come from people with some of the strangest advice for a mother who is hurting: "Do you have insurance on him? Make sure to take out a big policy." The longer he was gone, the more frustrated I became. I would ride the streets looking for him in the wee hours of the morning, desperately searching for my son, wondering who he was with, and how he was doing. Is he hungry? dirty? sick? What? I went so far as boldly walking into 'dope' houses looking for him. My hurt had turned into anger. Later, I learned that when we try to take things into our own hands, we hinder God from what He is trying to do. Finally, after days of my waiting and wondering, Dajuan came home.

Dajuan's Defiance of Authority

As a young, single parent, I used to say, "God help me! I don't know how to be a father to my boys." I tried, but I knew that no matter how hard I tried, I could never be the same as a father, and sometimes they resented the fact that I tried. I would play football with them, roast hotdogs and marshmallows, ride horses, wrestle and fish. I did the best I could with them.

Dajuan started football in the third grade and was very good at it. That was the time when I began to realize that DaJuan had a problem with someone telling him what to do. Teachers, principals and coaches were all of the same opinion. He had great potential, but he had a problem with anyone who had authority over him. He would even say so himself.

When Dajuan's second grade teacher asked me to come in to see her, I did. She showed me a drawing in his notebook; all he talked about was his father (who was barely in his life). A lot of what I saw was make-believe, but, what concerned me, was that there was not a word about me. I used to tell Dajuan, "You can draw so well; draw some mountains, trees, and flowers for me." Sometimes he would and sometimes he would not. Most of his drawings were of a man with a mean look on his face and a gun in his hand. Now as I look back, I recognize that there were all kinds of warning signals. I did not realize this until now. There was a seed of anger in him aimed at me because his dad and I were not together. My boys did not say it, but I knew that they felt that it was the woman's fault if there was no father in the home. That meant that it was my fault that their father was not in the home. Their thoughts seemed to be, "You had me, not him." Like a sore, pain can fester for years before it turns into anger and finally explodes. For my boys, it seemed that by puberty their hormones were fighting a period of identity crisis that boys go through. Their very hormones seemed to cry out for their fathers.

I found out later how Dajuan had become. No one told me that he was sneaking out and riding his bike all night while I was at work. I think that if someone had told me half the things he was doing, I would not have believed them. No, not Dajuan!

Problems with Dajuan in school grew worse. He was being suspended all the time. Finally, the district would no longer tolerate him and recommended that he attend the alternative school. The same thing happened there. He went from juvenile detention, to a group home, and from there to juvenile rehabilitation.

Now Dajuan is seventeen, and I cannot express the pain and suffering I feel when I hear gunshots almost every night, and I know that my son is somewhere out there doing wrong. Sometimes I find myself sitting in the window—stomach tied up in knots, knees weak, heart pounding—praying for protection and deliverance for my child. I try to maintain my faith in God to keep His Word, yet knowing that my son, controlled like a puppet by unseen forces, is somewhere standing on a corner where many have been killed. The devil is a liar. He will not have my son.

Dajuan eventually came home again.

God Gave Me Peace

God gave me a vision about my situation with Dajuan. In the vision, I saw a little girl fall and scrape her knee. She got up and ran to her daddy, who was sitting in a big chair. I couldn't see his face. He picked her up and put her on his lap, and everything was better. She was totally comforted by Him. What seemed like a crisis to her was only a scratch to her father. God told me that He was working on DaJuan's testimony and my not trusting Him was getting in the way. The situation with my son continues at the time of this writing. The difference now is that I realize God is working in my son's life in answer to believing prayer. I am learning more about faith with every moment that goes by.

A Wake-up Call

On June 26, 2002, at 2:30A.M., the two-and-a-half-year mark of our family prayer, I was at work when the phone rang. No supervisors were available to answer the phone, so the phone kept ringing and ringing. When it finally stopped ringing, I soon forgot about it. Little did I know that that phone call had been for me.

I left work at 6:30A.M., headed for Aunt Darlene's house to go walking. When I arrived, she told me to come inside. She said that she had been trying to reach me. I could tell immediately that something was wrong.

"Is it my kids?" I asked, and she said yes.

"Is one of them dead?" I asked. Thank God her answer was no.

"Are they in jail?" All I could think of was the worse for my sons.

"No, Dajuan is in the hospital," my aunt said. "It's not that bad. He was hit by a car." She named a broken hip and something about his arm. She had talked to someone at the hospital. I went home to get Aaron and we went to the hospital.

DaJuan was my seventeen-year-old, my baby. I knew that he was being controlled by the enemy, and all kinds of thoughts raced through my mind. At the time, I had been going through hell and high water with him. The devil had been having a field day with Dajuan, encouraging him to do everything he was big enough and bad enough to do. (Most of us have been there, too.) My prayer for Dajuan was, "God, do something before something bad happens to him. Give him a renewed mind, soften his heart, and save my baby, Lord. Even if You have to come down here, stop him in his tracks and set him down."

When we arrived at the hospital, we found out that Dajuan had suffered a broken hip and that his arm had been split open from the wrist to the elbow. It couldn't be sown up for three days because the exposed muscles and tendons were so swollen. His face was crushed from his eye to his jaw bone, and his mouth was

wired shut. He could not talk or walk. Dajuan went
through a lot, and so did I. He spent nine days in the
trauma ward, and I was at his bedside every night.

I thank God for saving Dajuan's life. He could
have been dead, but God had a plan, and it was already
working. Dajuan was on his back for about six weeks.
I had to blend all of his food everyday because he was
not yet able to eat solid food. He was in a brace from
his waist to his knee, and had stitches in his arm, mouth
and eye. The surgeon used titanium metal to hold the
bones together in his face. He underwent hip surgery to
repair the broken socket. God is good; He is so
merciful.

In the midst of what was happening to Dajuan, I
thought, "Well, this is his testimony; maybe he is going
to turn his life around." At this point in time, I don't
know where he is, but I do know what he is doing.
Confident that God would hear me, I prayed the
following prayer for Dajuan:

"God, please deliver Dajuan from anything and
everything that is not of You. Lord, send Your
ministering angels to encamp around him, to protect and
minister to him. Lord, place a hedge of protection
around him so that not one hair on his head is hurt.
Thank You, Lord. I close my eyes to the natural and
open them to the spiritual realm. Thank You, Lord, that
I can see him in the pulpit. I can see him doing the
things of God. I speak this into existence, in the Name
of Jesus. Lord, give him a clean heart and a sound mind.
Thank You, Lord; let it be done!"

I thank God that Dajuan is back walking, talking,
and living a normal physical life. I thank my family for
their support—just for being there for my son and me

everyday throughout the entire ordeal. I thank God for
my loved one; they are so dear to me.

Reflections

Until a short while ago, I was 39.999 years old.
This week I can hardly see what I am writing. Looking
back on four decades, I can see tragedy after tragedy and
triumph after triumph. If I could put all my tragedies on
a scale and weigh them against one triumph, the triumph
would outweigh the tragedy. The more you realize that
God has been with you all the time, just waiting for you
to call on Him, the more you can truthfully acknowledge
that He is alive and real. When you think about all that
you have been through, and that God was there all the
time, being whatever you needed Him to be at the
time—your comforter, healer, parent, friend, lawyer, and
provider—whatever you needed Him to be, He was just
that. God is so awesome.

I have always believed that life is what you make
of it, but sometimes we fail in making our life what it
should be. There is a reason why we are here on Earth.
We all have a purpose for being born. This is the reason
why we should seek the Lord so that He will reveal our
purpose in life. There is nothing on earth that can
compare to the presence of the Lord in your life. No
food, no drug, no sex—there is nothing that can compare
to supreme, ultimate intimacy with God.   When I
experienced His presence, I knew who I was, whose I
was, where I was, where I was going and from where I
had come. I came to this realization at the age of twenty-
seven, when I turned my life from destruction to
salvation.

The Battle of Infirmity
(Testimony of Aunt Darlene' Breast Cancer Trial)

First, I would like to explain my relationship with my Aunt Darlene, who is also the mother in my life. She and my Uncle Curtis raised me from a ten-year-old girl, and are still the parents in my life, and always will be. Aunt Darlene and Aunt Sharon, her sister, are like the flour, salt, sugar and yeast that hold the bread together and make it rise. They are like the aroma of the rolls cooking in the oven and the warmth of the rolls melting in your mouth—the ultimate pleasure of having them in my life. Being related to them is unspeakable joy.

I used to pray, "Dear God, please let me die before Aunt Darlene." I could not imagine being here without her. It seemed unbearable. Then one day she asked me to go to the doctor with her. She told me about the soreness under her arm and about the voice telling her it was cancer. Aunt Darlene rebuked that voice, but decided to have the sore spot checked out.

After running tests, the doctor wanted to do a biopsy. I knew I had to go with my aunt. I have always been tough as nails, but that day I turned in my resignation. I never showed it, but that news had done something to me. I thought to myself, "No, the devil didn't pull the cancer card out. He is trying to kill her." Satan was desperate to stop the attacks that we are putting on him. We fasted, prayed, rebuked the enemy, and bound his attacks. We began to rebuke curses and diseases off our family, binding on earth what has been bound in heaven (see Matthew 18:18).

Confidently, we went back to the doctor for the results of the biopsy. He took us into his office to inform us of the results. When he told us the tumor was malignant, I felt nothing—no fear, no tears—nothing I was completely calm. Peace is what I experienced— total peace. I probably had never felt peace like this before. A tear ran down Aunt Darlene's face. She later told me that one tear had been for her family, not herself. We acted as if the doctor's report had meant nothing. I just could not believe what the doctor had told us did not phase either one of us.

The doctor proceeded to tell us that my aunt had a fifty-fifty chance for survival. It was very small and caught at the earliest stage possible. He recommended she get a total mastectomy. "Why, if it's so little?" my aunt asked.

"You won't ever have to worry about it any more," he answered. "This is what most women are doing nowadays." He went on to say that the breast had no other significance other than breast-feeding.

When the doctor left, Aunt Darlene said, "I am not having my breast removed." I agreed with her. How could the doctor say that breasts don't have any other function than breast-feeding?

I told Aunt Darlene that I was going to tell the doctor's wife what he said (she was the receptionist). I further said to my aunt, "And when he comes back into the room, I'm going to tell him that testicles have no other function other than reproduction. When he is past producing offspring, is he going to get his testicles surgically removed?" (That's what I really wanted to say to him, but I didn't.) Anyway, she decided to have the cancer removed, but not the entire breast. After the procedure all that was left was a small indentation in her skin, and she is healed.

Through prayer, we have destroyed curses off our family. Aunt Darlene went through her battle with cancer so that no one else in our family ever will—the curse of cancer has been abolished. Her faith in the infallible Word of God brought us through. No one else in our family will have to experience cancer again.

Thank You, Lord, for my Aunt Darlene and Aunt Sharon. Their faith feeds us, the next generation. It causes us to rise closer to God like the yeast causes the dough to rise. Our faith, baked in the fiery trials we face, is transformed into something that has an aroma that touches something inside of us and makes us want more. "O taste and see that the Lord is good: blessed is the man that trusts in Him" (Ps 34:8).

A Dose of Reality

The summer of 1985 I was a twenty-three-year-old single parent of three boys, and I was destroying my life with drugs. My friends and several cousins were products of the sixties, and we almost naturally smoked pot and cigarettes. This was normal as far as we were concerned. This was life. Everyday we would gather at my house and play cards and dominoes and get high.

Let me explain. I had been on my own since I was seventeen years old. My father died when I was sixteen of a drug overdose. Someone had shot him up in the arm with aspirin and left him for dead. They had tried to make his death look like a suicide. When I was ten years old, my mother, fleeing an abusive marriage, left my three siblings and me with relatives. My brother

Chris and I moved in with our paternal grandparents. (I never saw my mother again until I was twenty years old.) Later, Aunt Darlene and Uncle Curtis became our parents. My two other brothers were given to other family members; therefore, my oldest and youngest brothers, Ricky (who died a tragic death) and Karriem, seemed more like cousins than brothers. Chris and I had always been together, other than when he went to the army. My older brother was a member of the United States Marine. As a matter of fact, all of my brothers were military men.

None of the unfortunate circumstances I have mentioned had anything to do with drugs *per se*. In reality, drugs became the weapons Satan would use to destroy my family. In the beginning, to me pot was a pleasure, not a need, but crack cocaine was a different drug. It was a form of demonic destruction sent from the enemy for one purpose—to destroy. The only way of escape this powerful addiction is to be delivered by God. Drug rehabilitation and counseling may help temporarily, but God, and only God, can truly deliver you. You must, by faith, turn to God for deliverance. God delivered me, and I never went back—never had the desire either. For me, that was nineteen years ago, and to my knowledge, my brother Chris and I are the only ones who have stopped using drugs. Chris has been *clean* for several years now, and that's a miracle. We owe our deliverance to God!

Let me tell you something that Satan does not want you to know. Nobody who is on crack cocaine wants to be on the drug. Those individuals addicted to crack are controlled solely by the drug like a puppet on a string. The ironic thing about using crack is that it's a joke. The first time you experience the drug, you get this electrifying sensation all through your body. Your heart is pounding at high speed. This is only the first time though. The first *hit* is a joke, and the joke is on you. You will *never* ever experience that feeling again—period. You will be teased from then on. Every time you smoke it, you think, just one more, and I will get that feeling, but it never happens.

Crack is highly addictive. When you put drugs into your system, you are opening the door for Satan to destroy you. Once the door has been opened, you expose yourself to all types of demonic activity. If you have never opened that door, don't open it! If you have opened it, seek the Lord for deliverance, *for only He can deliver you.*

My Day of Deliverance

I had my own house, and I had never gone back home after my son Nick was six weeks old. I did not begin using heavy drugs until my oldest son was six years old. Being on my own had taught me how to survive. Telling myself "I'm a survivor" is what kept me going. Not only did I provide for my children, but my brother Chris lived with me over a period of years until 1992. Then my other brother, Karriem, came to live with me for about a year. I never had my phone or utilities disconnected, and I successfully held my own with my children and was a good parent. I had never had a poor man's mentality. My thinking was that only the strong will survive. I would rely upon this strong will to survive one day when I overdosed on crack cocaine.

I had been smoking for three days straight without food or water, hating every moment of the sheer agony I was subjecting myself to, but I had no control—absolutely no control over my behavior. I had not slept or bathed in days. I was stuck in that chair in my living room, held prisoner by a demonic substance. Somehow, I *willed* in my heart to bring an end to this madness. I knew in my heart that only God could help me. My condition seemed hopeless (If you don't know Him, life can at times seem utterly hopeless.)

I was sitting there like a zombie—ninety-six pounds, hair falling out, very close to death. I had not eaten in three days. I had smoked so much crack that I went blind temporarily several times. I was awake and still talking, but I couldn't see. You would think that going blind, although temporarily, would have about scared anyone to death and they would have put the pipe down, but I didn't stop. I kept right on smoking, reaching for that moment of ecstasy. Then my jaws locked up—frozen shut. I could not pry open my jaws, even with my hands. I was trying to put a piece of bread into my mouth, but I couldn't open my mouth. The one good thing was that I couldn't open my mouth to smoke the pipe anymore either.

The person with whom I was getting high had left. I was now alone—just my pipe and me. As I lay on the couch, my body was dead weight. I could not move. My head was hurting so badly, and I could not cry or make a sound. My hand was lying on my chest, and I could feel my heart beating. My heart was beating so intensely that my hand was jumping up and slamming back down on my chest. My heart was beating so rapidly that I thought it was going to jump out of my chest. The pain in my head was so severe that if I moved my eyes or tried to squint, the pain would worsen. I realized that I was literally dying. At that moment, I cried out, "God, help me, please!" (I don't know whether or not the prayer was audible, or whether I spoke it in my heart.)

The last thing I remember thinking was, "I can't believe I went out like my father—on drugs." Instantly, I was standing over myself, thinking that I looked like an empty shell. At the same time I thought, "I'm over here, and my body is over there, but I don't feel pain anymore." Then I realized that I was dead. I had no normal reaction because I was still alive at the same time. There was no transfer of time between life and death. I tried to look down or to the side to see what the other body I was in looked like, or even if I were in a body like the one I had left, but I couldn't see it. My eyes were fixed directly on my body that lay on the couch—as if I were to study it and learn from it. This all happened within, I want to say seconds, but there is no time in the second life. Eternity is forever!

An image came up behind me and just stood. I was never in fear because I felt that whatever, or whoever, was there had come to help me. I could not think anymore. I was just there. I believe that a decision was being made whether to take me, or to give me another chance. Instantly, I was back in my own body— pain again, heart beating frantically—but I was alive again.

A voice said, "Roll off the couch and crawl to the bathroom." It was more like dragging myself because I was so weak. When I got in the bathroom a voice said to me, "Sit on the toilet and drink some water.

(Praise God, a cup was on the bathroom sink. Isn't God good?) I lifted the cup to my mouth to drink, and before I swallowed the water, I started to empty my bladder. I drank about ten cups of water and continually emptied my bladder. The more water I drank, the more I emptied the drugs from my system. It seemed that what went in came directly out. I felt that I was being cleansed and as I drank I began to feel energy building up inside me. Every cup of water I drank took me higher. My headache was now gone, and I was able to walk, holding on to the walls and doorway.

After my system had been flushed, I went to the couch, fell on my knees and prayed and thanked God. I did not fully understand what had just happened to me, but knew I had literally died and was brought back to life. God is real. He knew I had to absolutely know that for a fact—absolutely that He is real—before I would follow Him.

This was my prayer: "Lord, You know me, You know my heart, and You know I don't ever want to do drugs again. I'm not the mother I want to be for my sons, nor am I the person that I was. Lord, You know I've never been so serious in all my life. Thank You, Lord." At that moment, God delivered me. The desire to use drugs was gone. I cried on my knees before the Lord for two hours. I will never forget that day—the day God gave me another chance, the day that God delivered me from crack cocaine addiction. I prayed that I would do what He had purposed for me to do in this life.

All I could do was offer thanks to God for what He had done for me. *Thanks* seemed so little for so much that God had done in my life. I wish to offer this encouragement to anyone who is thinking of giving up on someone. Never give up, for God is always there waiting for you.

My Brother Ricky's Death

My two sons, two-year-old Nick and Aaron, who was seven months, were fast asleep. I had fallen asleep also. I do not remember how long I had been asleep before I was awakened by a dream that troubled me. I was so disturbed by the dream that I called Aunt Sharon and told her what I had dreamed. In my dream I saw the picture of a man naked from his neck to stomach. The frame was made of rolling clouds that appeared to be a window. I saw a fist reach out and hit the man in the chest, and at that moment, I woke up. As I was telling Aunt Sharon my dream, the other line beeped, and I put her on hold to answer the in-coming call.

The woman on the phone, identifying herself as a minister from Ohio, was asking for me. When I identified myself, she proceeded to tell me that my oldest brother, Ricky, had been killed. I thought the caller was one of Ricky's old girlfriends or somebody else trying to play a 'sick' joke on me, or something like that. I remember asking, repeatedly, "Who is this?" When the voice on the other end began trying to console me, I realized that the call was real. I threw the phone across the room and screamed. Hearing my screams, my friend came running into the room. Seeing me crying, he picked up the phone to see who was on the other end and then handed the phone back to me. The minister told me that Ricky had been in a fight and was stabbed in the heart three times. He died instantly. She informed me all his belongings had been packed in preparation to come back home. Ricky had just completed four years in the Marine Corps and had enrolled in school in Ohio to become a helicopter mechanic. But Ricky was not completely satisfied. The minister told me that Ricky had seemed restless, as though he had a 'monkey on his back.' He had told her that he was homesick and missed his family.

The last time I saw Ricky was the day he left for Ohio. I sat on the porch as he walked to his car. I said to him, "You are not coming back, are you?" He never said a word. He just turned, looked at me, and kept walking. (I miss my big brother.) I had always thought that he would come and get my two younger brothers and me after he had completed his time in the Marine Corps, and we would be a family again. I was twenty years old when my brother died.

Chris's Deliverance from Drugs

Chris and I are close. We grew up together. My older brother, Ricky, lived with our Grandfather Pollard, and my younger brother, Karriem, lived with Aunt Sharon. Chris and I were always together. Even when I moved into my own place, he lived with me. I was seventeen and Chris was sixteen. Nicholas, my son, was six weeks old when I moved into my own house next door to Aunt Darlene.

We lived in a rough part of the city where drugs were prevalent. We were like any other siblings, having knock-down-drag-outs and laughing and playing ten minutes later. Times were tough, but we had each other

other.It would not be long, however, before Chris would be engulfed in his environment. He began using drugs.

Later on, when drugs had taken Chris over, I knew I had to do something. He was controlled by drugs and thought he was invincible. He was doing things that no one in his right mind would ever do. I loved my brother so much, and I was willing to take the risk of his hating me in order to save his life—even if it meant having him committed to a rehabilitation center. He was very angry with me for having him committed, and he called me names. Having my brother committed was one of the hardest things I ever had to do, but I was afraid that if I didn't, he, too, would end up dead.

After he had dried out for thirty days, the rehabilitation center enrolled him in a program located in a little country town about five hours away. He decided to live there after his treatment had ended, knowing if he returned home, he would soon give in to the temptation of drugs once again. He did very well until he would come home for a visit. Then he would return to the same old crowd, and the nightmare would continue.

Chris was on the expressway to hell. Because of him, people were shooting at my house, threatening my kids and me. (By then I had three sons.) He was stabbed in the back of his thigh, and the wound severed his sciatic nerve. In attempting to explain Chris's injury, the doctor compared the nerve to the inside of a cable wire that has hundreds of nerves inside. He said it was impossible to reattach the nerve endings. The prognosis did not sound very promising. The doctor said that Chris would not be able to walk, and he would not have any feeling in his leg or foot.   Basically, what this meant was that he would be disabled for life.

One day Chris fell asleep on the floor, and his foot was lying over the heat vent. The heat from the vent roasted his toes like you roast hot dogs. (He had no feeling in his foot, so he was not aware of the damage that was being done to his toes.) His foot looked so bad that I just knew his toes would have to be amputated, but this was not the case. God again showed him favor, and there was no permanent damage to his toes.

We were so thankful that Chris's toes had been spared. Then God miraculously repaired the nerves in his leg. Chris had fully recovered from his wound. The devil had tried to cut him down, but Satan is no match for God, and we praise Him for His goodness. God is so good—all the time.

Years later, Chris told me that if I had not committed him to rehabilitation when I did, he would not have survived the lifestyle he was living. He would have been dead long ago. These events occurred years before our prayer group was established, but we had praying grandparents. The hand of God has been on us all our lives. Supported by a foundation of prayer built by our grandparents—true prayer warriors—we were not surprised when God called us to prayer. With God on our side, we would be unstoppable.

After we had begun praying for the chains of drugs and alcohol to be broken off our family, Chris came home and told me he did not have the desire to do drugs anymore, but he had to prove to himself whether or not this was true. He said he needed to hang around those same people with whom he had used drugs to see if he could endure the temptation. When he returned home, he told me that he still did not have the desire for drugs, and he knew that the change in his life had occurred because of our prayers. He was thanking us, but I told him to thank God for delivering him from destruction and death.

Of the ten people with whom we hung out and used drugs, Chris and I are the only ones who have been delivered from drugs. Hallelujah! Thank You, Lord! I have been drug-free for seventeen years; Chris, three years. I cannot imagine how the others manage to stay alive. I pray for them also, but they must want to change God will not override your will, but He will help you if you seek His help. I thank the Lord for delivering Chris and me from drugs and destruction. What the devil meant for evil, God is going to use for His glory to inspire those who have loved ones on drugs. They, too, can receive total deliverance, and the struggle will be over. All they need is to have faith in God the size of a mustard seed, and God will do the rest (see Matt. 17:20). I thank God for my brother, Chris, and we proclaim his salvation.

Trust Vision

One night, the Lord said to me to run bath water, light candles on each side of the tub, turn on the CD "Ribbon in the Sky," and turn out the lights. This may sound somewhat unorthodox to some, but I had nothing to lose. As I lay in the tub, the water was so relaxing that I fell asleep. This is the vision the Lord gave me that night.

I saw myself driving from the city to the country in total stress and turmoil. My mind was racing back and forth as I tried to deal with all the problems I was facing when I saw a field of flowers on a hill. I stopped. I was so distraught that I jumped from my car and ran over to a huge tree and sat down on the ground where I fell asleep.

The Lord came to me as I slept. He pulled my spirit from me by my hand, and my hand took His hand. We danced through the field of flowers to the song "Ribbon in the Sky," by Stevie Wonder. When God repeated to me the words to the song, I realized that this was what the Lord God was saying to me. I was so overwhelmed, so overjoyed—caught up to the highest of heights. Nothing earthly could compare to this feeling.

Then He guided me to the edge of the hill, which was actually the side of a mountain covered by clouds, so that you could not see the distance to the ground. I felt that the ground was such a long way down. The Lord guided me to the edge of the mountain, posing this question as we walked: "Do you trust Me?" I followed Him willingly a couple of times, but I would always stop short of the edge. He would keep on walking. I could not bring myself to step off the edge. The third time I stepped off the edge and discovered that I was standing on the clouds as if they were solid ground.

I had finally learned the lesson God was trying to teach me—to trust Him no matter how the situation looks. The Lord told me to remember this day. When I woke up, I was yet sitting by the tree, and I remembered everything that had happened.

When I obeyed the voice of God, I had no idea what was in store for me. I took a step of faith, and because of this vision, I came to trust God in a deeper way. Through one simple act of obedience, I had moved to a new level of trust in God.

Broken Vessel
(Karriem's Story)

My youngest brother, a thirty-five year-old sergeant in the United States Army, is the loving father of four and a single parent of two. Every day I thank God for him. When I am going through tough times, I think of him and his life's story, and my tough times don't seem so bad after all. At the age of four, Karriem, along with his sister and brothers, found himself without a mama to take care of him (earlier I stated that our mother left us because of an abusive marriage).

The three of us later moved in with our grandmother. After our grandmother passed away from cancer a year later, Karriem was separated from us. As a ten-year-old, Karriem would suffer yet another emotional blow—the death of our father. Our dad died unexpectedly at the age of thirty-seven. Although we had not seen our father for a few years, his death was no less devastating to all of us. A few years later, when Karriem was fourteen, our oldest brother was tragically killed. Within a ten-year period, he had lost several people dear to him.

Because of changes in the marital status of our aunts and uncles, Karriem was passed on to three different households within the family before he finally came to live with me. My situation was not the best. I was already struggling to take care of my three boys and our other brother, Chris. When Karriem came, I had to figure out how to stretch things (mainly food) even more. My inability to handle the stress in my life manifested itself in a terrible attitude towards my brother Karriem. Unable to deal with my negative attitude, he joined the army at seventeen.

The devil had stolen our childhood from us, starting with our parents and then our big brother, but we would not give in without a fight. When Karriem called me and said that he wanted to spend some time with me, I was so happy. We had been separated for years, but God would bring us together again. He was giving us another chance to restore our family ties. I thank God for His Word, which says, "And I will restore to you the years that the locust hath eaten . . ." (Joel 2:25a). God would restore the lost years.

In a short while, my "little brother" (Karriem) will be retiring from the army. He and I are about to take back what the devil stole from us. My brother recently bought a large boat, which he and I are going to restore. Then we're going fishing together. I thank God for keeping Karriem in good health over the years, both physically and mentally. He has never been addicted to drugs, nor has he been in trouble with the police. Others, under similar circumstances, may not have been able to endure the pain and suffering the devil sent our way, but, by the grace of God, my brother succeeded in life, in spite of the hardship he experienced as a child. He is my inspiration, and now the time has come for us to bond and enjoy life as brother and sister.

Restoring our family ties will be somewhat like the restoration of the boat which Karriem purchased. Just as the old 'broken' vessel will be stripped and scraped of all the sludge and corrosion from years in the water, so will the scars resulting from our broken relationship be stripped from us. The boat will be buffed, shellacked, and painted so that it looks as good as new. When the restoration is finished, it will be strong enough to withstand many storms to come. In like manner, the emotional storms which gad separated us years ago would no longer have power over us.

When the vessel is seaworthy, we will take it to the waters. The sail will be hoisted in the winds as my brother and I try our luck at fishing, a hobby common to both of us. We will reach out to each other in search of our future. Some of the experiences from the past have been painful and have left emotional scars, but our love for each other will help us erase the scars of the past so that we can go on with our lives. The Wind of God will blow upon us, lifting us above those things which hinder our fellowship.

Have you ever thrown your hands up and said, "Wind of heaven, fresh breath of God, breathe afresh upon me"? Did your hands become like a "skilled musician" as you listened to the "melody of heaven"? It is my prayer that God will breathe upon the relationship between my brother and me so that it will be restored as new. Just as we work at restoring this boat, my brother and I are determined to restore our relationship, and with God's help, we will. Everything that has been stripped will be renewed. We will both become vessels to be used of God in the seas of life and purpose. Every time a storm approaches, our arms will go up like sails in the wind to call upon my God. With my hands lifted toward heaven, I will bless the Lord all of my days.

Section IV

Tammy's TESTIMONIES

Speak to me, Lord....

My First Love

I was sixteen, a junior in high school, when I had my first child. I never knew love like this existed until I held my son Carlin in my arms. He was the most beautiful thing I had ever seen, and he brought me great joy. Were it not for divine intervention, I may never have experienced such joy.

The first thing my mom said to me when I told her I was pregnant was, "You are having an abortion." I did not have a choice in the matter. She scheduled an appointment and took me to Planned Parenthood to obtain information on the procedure. My mom scheduled a second appointment at which time the doctor would perform the procedure, but God intervened, because He had a different plan for my unborn son.

My mom went to church the Sunday before the procedure was to have been done, and she recommitted herself to God. This one act changed her mind about the abortion. I was not in the will of God when I became pregnant with Carlin, but my mom's decision to go back to church drastically changed our future. Because God had changed her heart, we started going to church regularly, and it was then that I realized I had to ask God's forgiveness for my sins also.

I had been out of school for three weeks, and after my son was born, my mom would go to the school every week to get all my homework assignments. She made sure I kept up with my work and did not quit school. I didn't know at the time what a blessing she was to me. My mom also paid for the baby-sitting, clothes, diapers, and took care of any other financial needs we had—all by herself. Carlin's father didn't help. After all, he was only nineteen and still a child himself. My mom carried the burden all on her own, with help and strength from God.

After I graduated from high school, I went on to college, taking evening classes, so I could make something of myself. My mom baby-sat for me four nights a week while I attended classes.

I loved Carlin with all my heart. He was the world to me. My mom provided for all our financial needs, I took care of Carlin myself, physically. Whenever he woke up at night, I cared for him, fed him and changed his diapers. As he grew older, he went everywhere I went, even on dates. I used to call him Buddy because he was my 'running buddy,' my friend.

Trouble in Paradise

Carlin began giving me problems when he was about seven years old in the second grade. He fought, talked back to his teachers, and refused to do his schoolwork. I was at his school constantly for meetings with his teachers or the principal. The problems only became worse as he grew older.

When Carlin was at Northwest Middle School, I was convinced that the teachers were the ones causing my son problems, not vice versa. We had experienced so many problems that I decided to transfer him to another school. There was a school out by mom's house that I thought would provide a better atmosphere for him.

I went to the school board and filled out all the necessary paper work to request a transfer. I had to give my mother temporary custody of Carlin for him to attend this school. In trying to be honest, I told them about the situation at Carlin's previous school. Of course, the administration at the receiving school was informed, so they knew that he was not supposed to be attending that school.

It wasn't very long into the school year that the same kinds of problems Carlin had at his previous school had resurfaced. He was skipping class, refusing to do his work, and talking back to his teachers—and the list goes on. By this time I knew that the real cause of the problems was my son and not the teachers. Carlin was expelled from that school—never to return. We had two choices—alternative school or back to Northwest. This time we chose Northwest. Carlin returned to Northwest, but the problems continued. Then we were given one final choice—alternative school.

I wasn't saved and living my life for the Lord when I was raising him and believe me it makes a difference. I tried reasoning with him and rewarding good behavior. I tried spankings and other types of punishments, but nothing worked. It wasn't until I was older and committed to the Lord that I learned that I should have been laboring in prayer for him.

Dream of Deliverance

One night I dreamed that I was standing in the doorway of my late grandmother's house (Mashan now lives in the house). There were tens and tens of teenaged boys walking through the front door. As they walked through, I anointed their heads and said, "In the Name of Jesus." They each came into the house and sat down. When I came to one of the boys whom I had anointed, he turned into a hideous monster. I wrestled him to the floor as I pleaded the blood of Jesus in spiritual warfare. After much labor, the monster turned into a baby, and I was sitting on the couch holding him. My dream had ended, and so had the struggle, and I was holding a newborn baby in my arms.

I told the dream to my cousin Mashan, who interpreted it for me. She informed me that all the boys who had come through the door represented the different spirits dwelling in my son, and that I was going to have to labor in prayer and warfare for his soul. The monster's turning into a baby represented my son's re-birth into the family of Jesus Christ. You can't imagine the joy I felt when Mashan told this to me.

God has revealed to me that I am now in the phase of laboring in prayer for my son Carlin's salvation, and the end is at hand. As of today, Carlin has not received the salvation of the Lord, but I stand on the Word of the Lord in the anticipation that he will be saved, and that his life will be a testimony for many young men who will come to the Lord because of it.

It is difficult to love a child who will not allow you to love him. But I love my son with all my heart. Often I have to remind myself to see him as the Lord sees him—to get a glimpse of the glory that is to come.

Once I found myself wide-awake at five o'clock in the morning. I asked God, "Whom do you want me to pray for?" I knew that I was in the part of my dream where I was struggling fiercely with Satan for my son's salvation. I began to pray for Carlin. I had been watching a television evangelist, and I recalled his saying if you pray the Scriptures, or in a prayer language, you will get results. God will answer your prayers. I began to pray God's Word back to Him regarding my son. I called out all the unholy things and began to bind on earth what God has already bound in heaven and lose on earth what God has already loosed in heaven. (See Matthew 16:19.) God has given us authority over all the power of the enemy, and I began to call on that authority, interceding for Carlin just as Jesus interceded for us in John 17:20-26.

As I lay in the bed praying, I thought about anointing my house, but I decided that I would do this when I got up. After all it was 5:30 in the morning. "No, get up and do it now," the Lord said. I got up and anointed everything I thought my son would touch— doors, doorknobs, faucets, the headboard on his bed, and even the toilet handle and seat. I also anointed my daughter.

Many times when I pray for someone, God will show me something about that person. This time, I saw Carlin, wearing a white robe in the pulpit and giving his testimony. I began to thank and praise God for saving my son. I fully expect that vision to come to pass.

I began to think about all the times in the Bible that God had "suddenly" showed up and delivered someone. I needed to see the manifestation suddenly. Carlin hadn't come home the night before. I wasn't worried, for I knew God's hand was on him. I just needed to see some results.

We had a guest speaker at church the following Sunday night. He told us to praise God for whatever we needed God to do in our lives. I immediately thought about Carlin and began to praise God as though Carlin were already saved. I shouted so loud and so long, I was exhausted when I finished. I probably was the loudest person in church that night. The evangelist also said that our prayers would be answered by morning. I fully expected to see the manifestation by morning.

I was so excited when I got home that night. Carlin was sleep and I didn't want to wake him.   I couldn't wait until Monday morning. I woke up with the same anticipation I had gone to bed with. When I came home from work that evening, Carlin was at home, but he was not the same Carlin. He began hanging around me, and this was very unusual.   I could tell that something was bothering him, and we had a long talk.

Carlin confessed that he was tired of his life the way it was, and that he needed a change. Carlin knew about God, but he just didn't know Him yet.   I told Carlin the only way his life would change would be for him to give all his problems to God. We got down on our knees to pray, and I lead my son into the salvation of the Lord. We both prayed and cried and prayed and cried.

We are still in warfare. Even though Carlin is saved now, I still have to continually pray for him. The enemy is still out to destroy him, but this will not happen. I know that God's hand has always been, and always will be, on Carlin. I know that the will of God will be done in Carlin's life, and that no weapon formed against him shall prosper. (Isaiah 54:17)

Old Things Become New

Looking back on my childhood, I have been able to put some things in perspective, but there are yet some things I do not understand. As a child, I was introverted. I closed out my family. I am not sure why. God had not revealed that to me yet. I felt contempt in my heart toward my sister and my mother. Maybe the reason was that I felt like my sister, Tiffani, was my mother's favorite child. I perceived that my mother was not able to show me the kind of love that she wanted to. It's ironic that I did the same thing my son has done to me— shut my mother out.

I always stayed in my room watching television or listening to music. I did not want to be around my family at all. I lacked confidence. Actually, I was very self-conscious and shy. I was also mean and hateful.

It wasn't until I was in my mid-twenties, when I recommitted myself to the Lord, that the hard, outer shell began to fall off. It was the love of God that changed me. His love will also change you if you will allow it to do so. I found that I could not confess to love God and hold contempt or hatred in my heart. As a result of our prayer group, I have grown closer to my mother and my sister than I have ever been. Now I can say that I truly love them both.

My sister called me the other day just to tell me she loved me. She has no idea what those three simple words did for me. That was the first time she had ever done anything like that. On the inside I was saying, "Oh, my God, this is a monumental moment. My sister called me to tell me she loves me. Oh, my God, I have to put this in the book."

Maybe my mother and my sister had loved me as a child, but I kept my distance and never allowed them the chance to prove it. What may have been, indeed, my imagination seemed real to me as a child. Now I welcome their love.

My First Home

I was twenty-six years old when I had my second child, Cortney, and I am still single. I was the mother of a son and a daughter, and I need not tell you the problems single parents face, because you probably already have some idea. However, I believe God allows circumstances to occur in our lives that will keep us running back to Him in times of great need. Being a single mother of two is one of them.

My children and I were living in a two-bedroom apartment. I wanted Cortney to have her own bedroom, so I began to look for a larger place to live. My mother had a friend who owned rental property, and it was just my luck that he had something available.

The house was located in the inner city. It did not look very good at the time, but it had potential. The rent was only $300 a month, and I had heard that the area school was much better than it had been in the past. I took it. The house would not have been my first choice, but, at that time, it was my only choice. I was a single mom with two children, and made a whole $8.10 an hour.

I liked the house in the beginning because it was a *house*. However, I soon grew tired of the noisy neighbors, the cars blocking my driveway when I came home from work, and the rare but existent sound of gunshots. I was raising my children in the ghetto, and this was not what I wanted. My daughter had no place to play and my son's only influence came from the other boys who hung out, got high on drugs, and had no regard for anything or anybody. I knew that I could not keep my family there any longer. I had been in that house for five years when I decided to move again. God had blessed me with a new job, and I was making about $13.00 an hour as opposed to the $8.10 I was making when I first moved.

I began making preparations to move. In five years you can accumulate a lot of "stuff." I began to sort through things, throwing some things away. I began to pack all the things I was going to keep. Six months before I moved, there were boxes stacked in the dining room with nowhere to go. I had not found a house. But God. . . !

It was income tax time and I had held on to my refund check for four months in search of a new home for my children and me. When I applied for a mortgage loan, I was pre-approved. I had looked at several houses, but I did not see anything I liked. One of my friends asked me, "Have you prayed?" Duh, no I hadn't.

Of course, as soon as I prayed, God heard and answered my prayer. I found the perfect house. An older couple had owned the house, and they had taken tremendous care of it. The house was in great condition. I didn't have to do any work prior to my moving in, except paint over the seventies-colored green, pink and tan walls throughout the house. It had three bedrooms, a full basement, an attached garage, central air-conditioning, and a big fenced in backyard where my daughter could play. The neighborhood was quiet, clean and peaceful. It was a gift from God.

I began making preparation to purchase the house. I knew I had to watch my finances because I wanted to be ready to close on the house when the time came. One Sunday morning during worship service, we had a guest speaker. At the end of the service the speaker asked for a certain number of people to give $1000.00. God spoke to my heart and told me to give the $1,000. I said, "God, I can't give that money! That's my house money." He told me to give it anyway. I was obedient, so I wrote out a check for $1,000—the most I had ever written a check for in my life. I had to tell the deacon not to cash the check immediately so I could transfer the funds from my savings account.

When the time came for me to close on the house, I didn't have the money. The title company called to set up a date and time for me to sign the mortgage papers, but I did not have the money. I called the bank to see if it had money set aside for situations such as this. I had asked that question at the bank before and the response was no. This time, however, the bank was able to find funds for me. I also called the agency where I had taken my home-buyers class and discovered that there were closing-cost monies available to those who had participated in the class.

After signing my life away at the title company, I walked away with a check payable to me. I had more money than I needed for the closing costs. We serve an awesome God—One who will do exceedingly, abundantly above all we can ask or think (see Eph.3:20). There aren't too many days when I walk through the house and I don't thank God for His blessing.

Visions

During our prayer time, I usually pray for spiritual gifts—wisdom, knowledge, and revelation. I also pray for love and peace. I pray in this way because I always want to be aware of what God is doing in our lives, and I want us to be mindful of what God expects of us.

It is during prayer that God reveals things to me. One of the things God showed me was how He has kept tragedy from our loved ones. I once saw God's hand pouring out the blessing of safety from danger and injury upon our family. He let me know that our prayers produced a pleasing aroma in His nostrils. When God heard our prayers, He stopped what He was doing and said, "There go those Minor Girls again," and He answered our prayers. The Word lets us know that when we speak well of Him, he listens and writes it in a book of remembrance. (See Mal. 3:16.)

We were expecting to see the miracle of salvation happen over and over again in our family. We cannot even begin to imagine what God has in store for us, not only in this life, but also in the life to come. Our prayers have moved the hand of God over our family to bless us, to protect us, and to let us know that He is ever present with us. We thank Him for the miracles yet to come.

Parenting with Prayer

Raising children, even with two parents in the home, has become more difficult nowadays than in the past. You can imagine what it's like raising children as a single parent. I have already told you about the problems I experienced with my son. My daughter, Cortney, from pre-school through third grade, had been an ideal student. Her grades were excellent—straight A's—and all of her teachers loved her, and for this very reason, I didn't cover her in prayer as I should. When Cortney entered the fourth grade, things began to change. She began exhibiting behavior totally out of character—back talking her teachers, playing around, and refusing to stay on task. As I began to survey the situation in the spirit, I hated what I saw, and I did not even want the words to come out of my mouth. God had revealed to me that Cortney was under satanic attack.

Our prayer group met at Aunt Darlene's house the same week that God had revealed to me what was happening to Cortney. When I told my aunt what was going on with my daughter, she immediately took authority in the Spirit and began to bind that attack of the enemy and to release positive behavior into Cortney's life. I received a much better report from Cortney's teachers the following week. I was reminded to pray for my daughter as often as I prayed for my son.

His Chosen

God's hand has always been over my life. Even when I was living life outside the will of God, His divine protection hovered over me because of the prayers of my sainted great-grandparents. Our coming together—the six of us—was no accident. All of us have been chosen, anointed and ordained to pray for our family. God has also told me that my daughter will follow in my footsteps and do even greater things. He reminds me to pray for her always.

In the past, I spent more time praying for my son, Carlin, than I did for Cortney because he had not accepted Jesus as his Savior. Because I knew that my daughter had the call of God on her life, I sometimes neglected to pray for he. This was exactly the reason why I needed to pray for her more fervently. Although I was single, I had earnestly tried to bring up my children in the way of the Lord according to Proverbs 22:6: "Train up a child in the way he should go: and when he is old, he will not depart from it." I claimed that verse of Scripture for both my children.

Being a single parent causes much frustration sometimes. Because I bear the weight of parenting alone, I sometimes grow weary in my body and spirit. I work all day on the job and come home and work more—cleaning the house, doing laundry, buying the food and cooking it too, mowing the grass in the summer, raking the leaves in the fall, and shoveling snow in the winter. I do it ALL. In addition to taking care of my home, I try to be faithful to my church, and I am in the process of starting my own business. Oh, did I forget something? I also pay all of the bills. Sometimes, I just want to give up. There have been times when I would just lie in the bed and cry. I probably would have given up, had the Lord not comforted me through His Word. I relied frequently upon this verse of Scripture: "Thou wilt keep him in perfect peace, whose mind is stayed on thee: because he trusteth in thee" (Is. 26:3). I have this verse on a post-it note on my computer at work.

Do I sound as if I am complaining? I am by no means complaining. I thank God that I have a house in which to do the things I mentioned. That was my attempt to paint a picture of what my life is like as a single parent. You are responsible for everything, including the disciplining of your children—even if they are boys. If you are single and you are reading this book, I'm sure you can identify.

I am convinced that God will not allow you to suffer more than what you are able to bear. Whenever I get to the end of my rope, or when my rope begins to frazzle, God always reaches down and rescues me. God has sent us a Comforter, the Holy Spirit, and He will keep us in perfect peace. At that moment when the enemy tempts us into believing that no one cares, God will send someone to cut the grass for me or shovel the snow. He blesses my finances so that I can sometimes treat myself to dinner out instead of cooking. Whenever I need some quiet time alone, I allow Cortney to spend time with her father. There are times when I have to encourage myself by saying, "Wow, Tammy, you're thirty-six years old, and you own your own home! That's a major accomplishment for a single black woman with two children." Everything I do— everything I have accomplished—I have done it by the strength of the Lord, who has breathed His blessings upon me.

When I turned thirty-six, I found myself having to psyche myself up for facing this birthday. I had passed the mid-point and was closer to the age when, according to popular belief, "life really begins." I told myself this was going to be a good birthday. I must admit that I had been just a little upset about turning thirty-six, and being single and not having anyone to share my birthday with other than my family. Don't misunderstand me. I love my family dearly, but there are times when having a man in your life would make *b-days* more special.

Driving to work the morning of my thirty-sixty birthday, trying in every way I knew to psyche myself up so that I would have a great birthday, God began to show me what He has spared me from. First of all, He had spared me from being in an unhappy relationship. Second, He had spared me from a relationship with someone who would not love me the way I deserve to be loved. Thirdly, God had spared me from being in an abusive relationship. Finally, He had spared me the pain of feeling unwanted and unloved. I immediately began to thank God and praise God for having had mercy on me and saving me from having to endure the hardship of an unhealthy relationship. When God chooses to place a man in my life, he will follow the advice given by Paul in Ephesians 5:25 and 28: "Husbands, love your wives, even as Christ also loved the church, and gave himself for it. . . .So ought men to love their wives as their own bodies. He that loveth his wife loveth himself."

The Call

I remember the day God spoke to me about my calling to preach the Gospel. I had been talking to my friend Patrice on the phone. She was my spiritual mentor, my spiritual sister, and my best friend. God had always used her to confirm things in my life and to guide me in the right direction.

When I spoke to her on the phone, I never used the word *preach*. That was above me. I could not be a preacher. As the conversation continued, trying to explain my calling to Patrice in a roundabout way, I told her I was going to be a speaker and a writer. Her response was, "I know. I have known for quite some time." I don't remember much after that, dropping the phone, falling out on the bed, and praising God. That was in April of 1998.

I can remember thinking, "How could God choose me? I was quiet, shy and introverted. I was scared to death of appearing in front of people. How could I possibly stand up in front of church and 'speak'? It took me about two years to tell my pastor. As time passed I felt a sense of urgency to answer the call. I did not want to be found failing to fulfill God's purpose for my life.

When I talked to my pastor and told him about the call of God on my life, he was not surprised. As a matter of fact, he was quite tickled about the whole thing. I had been attending his church since I was fifteen. He told me he felt as if he were having this conversation with one of his daughters. As we talked he analyzed verses of Scripture pertaining to the call to ministry. We concluded with prayer. I left his office with the assignment to write a paper on "Why I Feel I've Been Called."

A couple of weeks later, I returned to the pastor's office with assignment in hand. Immediately after reading my paper, he scheduled tentative dates for my first message. At the same time, I would be announced as a new *aspiring missionary*. "Missionary," I thought. "Whoa, hold it! That's way too fast for me.

What? Missionary? Where did the title come from? You mean you are actually going to call me missionary? All I want to do is God's will. I don't want a title with it." (Our church does not refer to women as *preachers*; it uses the term *missionary* to refer to women who carry the Gospel.)

The title was an issue within in itself, one that I would have to deal with, in addition to accepting the responsibility of the call. I was able to view the title as part of God's purpose for my life. I prayed and asked God to give me the mind to accept not only the title but also the responsibility that comes with the title. Presently, I am growing and learning how to walk in this awesome responsibility.

I have been writing for as long as I can remember. I love to write. I have collected papers and writings from the time I was in elementary school. As I grew older, the writing changed. I remember at some point thinking, "These surely sound like sermons." I had no idea at the time that some of those papers would, indeed, turn into sermons.

I have grown quite a lot spiritually in the last five years. I have come to the realization of *who I am* and *whose I am* in Jesus. I am no longer introverted. I have learned to look my fears dead in the face and know that "I can do all things through Christ which strengthens me"(Phil 4:13). When I encounter fear, I claim God's Word: "For God has not given us the spirit of fear; but of power, and of love, and of a sound mind" (II Tim. 1:7).

Although I received the call to ministry in April of 1998, it was spring of 2000 that I delivered my first message. I was one of those that God could only reveal a little at a time, or else I might take off running in the opposite direction. I greatly rejoice that I have accepted the title, the call and the responsibility that accompanies it: God did not *cal l me for such a time* as this without *equipping me for such a task as this*. He has invested much of Himself in me, and to "whomsoever much is given, of him [her] shall be much required. . . " (Luke 12:48).

Section V

Tiffani's TESTIMONIES

Lord, I humble myself before You... I want to be pleasing in Your sight...

Walking in God's Favor

The year 1994 was a year of testing for me (Tiffani). Everything seemed to hit me in the face at the same time. In the midst of going through a divorce, I changed jobs, and began looking for a house. In February my two sons and I had moved in with my mother and stepfather. Picture a four-year-old, a two-year-old, and myself sharing a 14' x 13' bedroom! That was probably the longest five months of my life.

My divorce became final in June. The summer of 1994, I found myself a twenty-four-year-old single mother with two boys to raise. I felt hurt, disappointed, rejected, and betrayed in every way. I felt like a complete failure, but God gave me grace to keep moving forward. As I look back over that time in my life, I know that I was living totally off God's grace.

I had begun looking for a house as soon as I moved in with my parents. At that time, I wasn't even making $20,000.00 a year. I had just bought a new car the fall of 1993, had two boys to take care of, and I was in search of a new home. I had been pre-approved for a mortgage loan, and the search was on. However, finding a house I liked in the price range for which I had been approved was a little difficult. I definitely didn't want to raise my boys in the 'hood.'

One day as I was driving through a sub-division, I saw the cutest little house. I remember thinking, "I can't afford that," so I never mentioned the house to my realtor. We had probably looked at three or four houses that I didn't like at all before I mentioned the little house I had seen on the corner of Sixty-second and Nebraska. After I had called the realtor and told her about the little corner house, she checked on the price and set up an appointment for me to see it. It was listed exactly for the amount for which I had been approved. I was so excited and could not wait to see inside the house. When I walked in, I knew that it was the one. We began filling out the contract, and I was on my way.

Forty-five days passed. All the paperwork had been delivered to the underwriter, and I was just waiting for my closing date. Then I received a rather disappointing phone call that would send me searching for a house one more time. The lady on the phone informed me that I had not been approved for the full amount. The bank would only give me a loan for two-thirds of the amount I needed. My heart dropped. I simply did not understand what was going on. I said, "But I was pre-approved for—." The lady interrupted me, trying to explain what had happened. My pre-approval for a loan had meant nothing.

I had taken my friends by this house, and my friends were taking other people by the house, telling them it was mine. I couldn't believe that this was happening to me. I had expressed to God that I didn't want to be a single black mother raising my two boys in the 'hood' because of so many negative influences. That had been a strong desire of my heart.

I wasn't ready to give up. For me it was back to the drawing board. Now I had to find a lower-priced house that was not located in the 'hood.' I had probably looked at two or three more houses before I received a phone call from my realtor. She called to let me know that the house I had wanted was still available. The owners' children had made the decision to pay off the second mortgage on the house, which, believe it or not, totaled the difference I needed. The Lord had honored my prayers by blessing me with the house I wanted, and it wasn't in the 'hood.' The house had everything I was looking for: three bedrooms, one and a half baths, a one-car garage and siding. (I would not have to worry about painting the exterior.) The Lord even added a bonus blessing. Not only did I get the house for my pre-approved amount, but I also received a grant that further reduced the loan amount needed. I moved into my new house on the first of July. To God be the glory!

My ex-husband had always been extremely athletic. As a teenager, he excelled in track, even going to the Junior Olympics a few times. He also holds a black belt in jujitsu, and once was approached for professional kick-boxing. When he broke his neck playing semi-professional football, he turned to me during his convalescence. As a result, after two years of being divorced, we remarried.

One evening after dinner, my husband and I sat down and wrote a list of everything we wanted in our new home that we were dreaming of buying. I placed the list in my Bible and would look at it periodically. Since I was off work, I had lots of time to think. In May of 1999, the idea came to me that we should apply for a loan to purchase a house. I thought it was a bright idea, even though I was not working and had no salary. The house we wanted was in an ideal location, several miles from the inner city. We were approved and started the process of securing a loan. The process did not run smoothly at all. I could not understand what the hold-up was. Our credit rating was fine. Eventually, I became frustrated and gave up on the program.

Approximately four months later my husband and I decided to sell the house in which we were currently living. By this time our family prayer group had been organized. I asked my prayer partners to agree in prayer with me that we would sell our house within thirty days, and that we would receive the amount of money we were asking. We sealed this prayer request with one of our favorite verses of Scripture: "Again, I tell you that if two of you on earth agree about anything you ask for, it will be done for you by my Father in heaven" (Matt. 18:19 NIV).

My husband and I put our home on the market, and the realtor ran all of the statistics for the sub-division where we lived. According to her information, houses in our area were requiring sixty plus days to sell. In addition, we were asking $10,000.00 more for our house than the price for which the other houses in the neighborhood were selling. When our realtor suggested that we lower the price, I said no. Over the five-year period that I had been in the house, I had totally remodeled it, and the house looked great. I would not settle for a price lower than what I thought my house was worth.

Once again the Lord honored our prayers. The house was on the market for only six days. The very first weekend the realtor showed the house, it sold. God blessed us to receive the amount we had asked for, and the house had sold in less than a week's time. We grossed more than twice the price we paid for it. After paying off everything we were living debt free. Because the house sold so quickly, we had to move in with my parents for a few months, until we found a place to live. Later, we found a duplex in suburban Kansas City. Six months after we had moved into the duplex, I found a full-time job through a temporary (temp) agency.

When we began to look into buying a new home, I was told by two mortgage companies that I could not get a loan working for a temp agency. Not long after having received that terrible news, I was riding around helping my parents look for a new house. A realtor at one of the model homes gave me a business card for one of the mortgage companies that she frequently used (things don't just happen). I called the loan officer that next Monday, explained that I was trying to get a pre-approval, and that I was presently working for a temp agency. He went on to assure me that my current job status was no problem. We were pre-approved, and we started searching for a new home.

Our search for a new home was exciting. As we rode through the city, there was one particular neighborhood that I especially liked. The area was visible from the highway, but we had never stopped to look at the homes. Every time we would pass the area, I would always say, "We can't afford to live over there." Little did I know what God had in store for us. Three months after we had started the process of finding our new house, God blessed us to move into that very neighborhood that I had previously felt was too expensive for us to even look at. The value of our new home was double the amount of the lower-income house we had been trying to get. That experience taught me never to put God in a box.

Two months after we moved into our new home, my job laid me off. Once again there was a tremendous drop in our income, but once again, God provided for us. Not once have we missed a mortgage payment. God has taken care of all of our needs according to His riches in glory. God gave us way more than what we had requested on our list of things we wanted in our house. I didn't even think to ask Him for most of the pleasures and conveniences He gave us in our new home. For example, all I had asked for in my master bedroom was a bathroom. Not only did He give me a bathroom, but He also gave me a double vanity, a jacuzzi, a separate shower, and his-and-hers walk-in closets. Not only had God provided my needs, but also He had given me something extra. We were walking in His favor, and we were reaping what He has said in His Word: "And my God will meet all your needs according to his glorious riches in Christ Jesus" (Phil. 4:19 NIV).

God does stand by His Word to perform that which He has spoken:

> *Ask and it will be given to you; seek and you will find; knock and the door will be opened to you. For everyone who asks receives; he who seeks finds; and to him who knocks, the door will be opened* (Matt. 7:7-8 NIV).

> *Now to Him who is able to do immeasurable more than all we ask or imagine, according to His power that is at work within us"* (Eph. 3:20 NIV).

God will do "exceeding abundantly above all that we ask or think" (Eph. 3:20) when we fix our faith on Him.

A Daughter's Cry to God

It was wintertime in 2000, and my mother called me to let me know that she would be leaving work and going to see her doctor.   Earlier, the doctor had instructed my mom to pick up a prescription for insulin prior to the office visit so that the doctor could show her how to self-administer her insulin shots. (My mom has already shared this testimony, but I want to express how I felt in this process.) The very thought of my mother having to give herself a shot everyday pierced my heart. I just couldn't imagine her having to give herself a shot everyday for the rest of her life. Why was this happening? I knew the answer. We were interceding for our family, and Satan was on the attack.

I called my Aunt Darlene and told her what was going on with my mother and stated that we needed to pray right then. When I hung up the phone I fell on my face before the Lord. I prayed, cried and wailed before the Lord on behalf of my mother, requesting of God to heal her so that there would be no need for her to inject herself with insulin everyday. The Lord let me know that he would heal her.

Later that day my mother called to give me an update. By the time she had arrived at the doctor's office, her blood sugar count was down. As a matter of fact, the reading had dropped so much lower than it had been earlier that day that the doctor advised my mother that she would not need insulin injections, but that she could control the diabetes with medication and diet. I give God all the praise. That day the Lord increased my faith more than a little. What a mighty God we serve!

A Father Absent

My father passed when I was twenty-nine years old. His death brought to the surface so many things about myself that I had concealed for so many years. I felt that I had missed so much by not having him in my life constantly when I was growing up.

My mother and father divorced when I was about nine years old. When he left, a piece of me left with him. When my mother finally put my father out, I just couldn't understand why she had done that. She would never talk bad about him. Whenever we questioned her about our dad, she would say, "You will understand when you get older."

I did not really understand the circumstances which had caused my parents to divorce. All I knew was that I missed my father. I expressed my loss in ways that made sense to me. I would cry and pretend to be sick so I wouldn't have to go to school. My mother said I would do that just to stay home and torture her about putting my father out. She said I would say things such as, "Are you happy now?" to punish her for sending my father away.

My father really did not interact with me on a regular basis during my teenage years. Once I graduated from high school, however, we talked more. I knew that my father loved me, but he had a 'not-showing-it' way of expressing his love toward me. He would always say, "You are beautiful, and I love you," but the actions did not follow the words.

A special time with my father occurred when I was twenty years old. One day my father called me. He and I were just having small talk, reminiscing about my childhood, when he admitted that he was sorry for having missed out on my teenage years, and that he regretted not having been there. One part of me felt good because my father was experiencing pangs of guilt. I wasn't prepared to deal with what the other part of me felt. It was buried too deeply in my childhood.

As a little girl, I needed to be nurtured and loved by my father. The absence of a father in a young girl's life could have negative effects on her adulthood. Because my father was absent during my adolescent years, I found myself searching for love, and never being able to find love to the extent that I needed it. Have you ever heard the saying that a girl tends to marry a man just like her daddy? Well, in some ways, I did just that. I married a man who said that he loved me, but he had a difficult time showing it on a daily basis.

I knew that I would never be able to recapture the time I had missed being with my father, but I was with my father when he died. I watched him die. For about a week I had been with him at the hospital daily. In the beginning he had been able to talk a little, but after a couple of days that changed. He would try to talk, but he just couldn't get any complete sentences out.

One day he and I were left alone in the room. With tears in my eyes, I asked him, "Daddy, do you love me?" As he nodded, yes, he was trying to tell me something, but I couldn't understand him.

I asked, " Why didn't you show me when you could?" This time he did not try to speak. He looked at me sadly as a tear rolled down his face.

My father passed a couple of days later. I felt cheated. I had unanswered questions I felt only he could answer. My father had abused his body, and as a result of that, he died at the young age of fifty-one.

Five years have passed since my father died. Finally, I am open to forgiving him for abandoning me. It hasn't been easy, but through prayer and talking to God about it, my healing has begun.

One Thursday night prayer was held at my house. At the end of prayer we formed our circle, holding hands as usual. I stood in the middle of the circle. My sister started the prayer, praying for my family and me. Aunt Darlene followed, and Mashan finished the prayer. As she prayed, Mashan asked God to heal that hurt, broken teenage girl inside me. Her words took me immediately back to my father. I began to cry. Mashan went on to say, "God wants to heal all the hurts of your past concerning your father so you can be complete." She saw a vision of me holding my broken heart in a box, giving it to God. When I gave the box to Him, God asked, "What took you so long to give it to me?" Mashan recalled a similar encounter with God concerning herself, and seeing me giving God the box had brought the incident back to her remembrance. I realized that I needed total healing in this part of my life so that I could give love in order to receive love in return.

Before the 'I Dos'

If I haven't learned anything else in life about marriage, I have already learned the most important thing: Don't be unequally yoked! Before contemplating a marriage partner, everyone should heed the words of the apostle Paul recorded in II Cornthians 6:14-15 (NIV):

> *Do not be yoked together with un-*
> *believers. For what do righteousness and*
> *wickedness have in common? Or what fellow-*
> *ship can light have with darkness? What*
> *harmony is there between Christ and Belial?*
> *What does a believer have in common with an*
> *unbeliever.*

A person can say that he or she is saved, but the real question is, "Does he or she have a relationship with the Lord?" There is a difference between being 'saved' and having a 'relationship' with the Lord. A lot of times we look at such behaviors as church attendance every Sunday, knowledge of the Bible , listening to gospel music 'sometimes,' and—don't leave this one out—being raised in the church.

To ascertain whether or not a person has a relationship with God, you must watch the way that person talks—is it spiritual, or is his mind always on worldly or sensual pleasures, such as sex? Do you see him or her pray regularly? If the individual is a man, how does he treat his mother? Does he treat her with love and respect? Do you see him read the Word? Does he believe in tithing? How does he feel about rearing children in this day and time? What are his priorities when it comes to the Lord? Does he suggest prayer before making decisions? Don't allow yourself to get caught up in his seemingly knowing something about the Lord, but fast and pray so that God will show you the truth about the individual. You will be glad that you followed this advice in the long run. The only way that a man will know how to treat the jewel God has given him is to have an intimate relationship with God.

Marriage is hard work, but it is even harder when two people are unequally yoked. The type of lifestyle in which you will find yourself definitely will not be fulfilling, and such a life can also be very miserable. When you make the decision to spend the rest of your life with a person whom God did not choose for you, you set yourself up to experience many trials and disappointments that could have been avoided had you only stopped and sought the Lord with all your heart long before you said, " I do" at the altar.

If you have detoured from God's original plan for your life and find yourself in this situation—married to someone who claims to know the Lord, says that he is saved, but very clearly shows no fruit of salvation— don't despair. You may have been praying for his or her deliverance and it seems as if things are only becoming worse, by faith, grab hold to the message of the parable spoken by Jesus in Luke 18:1-8 (NIV).

> *[1] Then Jesus told his disciples a parable to show them that they should always pray and not give up. [2] He said: In a certain town there was a judge who neither feared God nor cared about men. [3] And there was a widow in that town who kept coming to him with the plea. 'Grant me justice against my adversary.' [4] For some time he refused. But finally he said to himself, 'Even though I don't fear God or care about men, [5] yet because this widow keeps bothering me, I will se e that she gets justice, so*

that she won't eventually wear me out with her coming!' [6] *And the Lord said, 'Listen to what the unjust judge says.* [7]*And will not God bring about justice for his chosen ones, who cry out to him day and night? Will he keep putting them off?* [8] *I tell you, He will see that they get justice, and quickly. However, when the Son of Man comes, will he find faith on the earth?"*

The moral of this parable is that we should always pray to the Lord and never give up. A judge that had no respect for God or man honored this woman's request because she diligently sought him.

The Lord wants us to realize that He is our heavenly Father, and that He loves us. He will do as the 'unjust judge' did and even more. We should be tenacious in praying for our spouses—that they will be the persons that God intended them to be.

God's Revealing Gift

It was mid-December and very mild outdoors for winter. I decided to take advantage of the warm weather and visit a close friend whom I had known most of my life. Before I left her apartment, we had prayer. My friend prayed first and I followed. After I had finished my prayer, she told me that God had given me a gift to pray prophetically. He wanted to increase this gift in my life so that I would not be afraid to speak into existence what I would hear or see. I looked at her as if to say, "Just what are you talking about?" My friend proceeded to explain to me that God would show me future events in someone's life, and I was to pray and speak what I had seen or heard. What she had said did not register at first, but I received what she had told me. I had lots of time to think about what my lifelong friend had said during my long ride home.

A couple of weeks later, the Lord dropped into my spirit to pray and speak that God would bless Shontelle, my cousin, with a permanent job before the end of the year. I procrastinated and did not tell Shontelle right away. By the time we met for prayer again, I was ready to exercise the gift God had given me. That week at prayer I told Shontelle that I would agree in prayer with her that the Lord would bless her with a job before the end of January. She responded with an O.K. I had been reluctant to speak what I had heard God say, with the end of the year almost upon us.

The word that God had given me concerning Shontelle weighed heavily on my mind. I had to be obedient and speak what God had revealed to me. I e-mailed Shontelle and told her that I would agree with her in prayer that the company for which she worked would offer her a permanent position before the end of the year. She responded again, "O.K."

On December 30, Aunt Darlene, Tammy, my mother (Sharon), and I were sitting at my mother's house when my aunt's cellular phone rang. It was Shontelle. My aunt was smiling and saying, "For real!! For real!!" The rest of us were asking, "What? What? What?" By Aunt Darlene's reactions, we knew that the news was good. I will allow Shontelle to share the rest of this testimony, but I will say that her supervisors did let her know that her job would be permanent.

One of the things that we have prayed for during our weekly prayer is that God will reveal our purpose to us, and that we will be receptive and walk in the purpose He has ordained for us. He is doing just that.

'Between' the Six of Us

Our prayer group has meant so much to me. God has tightly knitted us together in the past three and a half years. If I have a burden that is too heavy for me to carry alone, I can always pick up the phone and call Tammy, Mama or Aunt Darlene and know that they will pray immediately. It's a wonderful feeling knowing that I have a family that genuinely cares for me I can go to them in times of need. Whenever I have a problem, I can go to them, and they won't put my business in the street. Instead of talking about me, they will honestly take my situation to the Lord in prayer. .

We cry together, rejoice together, praise God together, laugh together, dance together, and pray together. There is so much love shared between the six of us, and it is this love, and the help of God, that helps me through the rough times in life. I thank God for allowing me to be a part of this circle of prayer.

A Prayer from the Heart

The Lord has impressed upon my heart many times to pray this prayer on behalf of my family:

> *Dear God, I thank you for my family, and for calling me to intercede for their salvation, deliverance, and relationship with You. God, I ask, according to Your Word, in the Name of Your Son Jesus Christ, that You remove the*

veil of darkness from their eyes so they can see the glory of the Lord and Your Truth.

Lord, I pray that You pull down every stronghold that causes them to sin against You. I pray that they become uneasy when they sin against their own bodies and against You.

Lord, send your ministering angels to them right now. Prepare their hearts and minds to receive Your Word. I pray that the seeds planted in them fall on good ground, and that they will not allow Satan to steal the seed that is planted.

Lord, I pray that You arise in every situation—mine and theirs—and let Your authority and power be known. I pray this prayer in the blessed Name of Jesus. Amen.

Section VI

Shontelle's
TESTIMONIES

Lord, I thank You
for answering my prayers....

The Baptismal Pool Incident

From my youth, I (Shontelle) have known that God would protect His children from danger. I can remember very vividly one incident in which God manifested His presence to save me from a terrible accident in the basement of my church. I was a little girl in elementary school. We held Sunday school classes in the basement, and sometimes the children would play during the break between Sunday school and morning worship. Little did I know that morning that danger was lurking in the basement.

That morning was sunny outside. I remember the sun shinning through the basement windows. Most of the people had cleared the basement, but I continued to play as I waited for my mother to come downstairs and get me for church. I skipped along the concrete floor, unaware of the open in-ground baptismal pool in my path. As I was about to make the next step down, I glanced with my peripheral vision and saw the baptismal pool. I felt myself leap over the pool and land on the other side. As I was airborne, it seemed as if I were gliding over the pool in slow motion, yet everything happened so fast. When I landed I was shaken up. I stood there reflecting on what had just happened. Even as a child, I remember thinking that it must have been God who had carried me over the pool.

I took a good look at the pool, and I could not believe I had made that jump. I don't know how wide it was, but, in retrospect, the jump seemed almost impossible, especially since I really had not been aware of the pool being there. After my unexpected leap, one of the ladies of the church cautioned me not to play near the baptismal pool because I could injure myself. The pool must have always been covered before. I remember thinking, "I didn't even know it was there, so I wasn't trying to jump over it." Actually, I did try to tell her, but she didn't pay any attention to what I was saying.

I often think about what happened to me that day. As I grew closer to the Lord and began developing my relationship with Him, I began to understand the kind of God we serve. I believe with all my heart, mind, and soul that the Lord lifted me up that morning and carried me over that baptismal pool to the other side. Now a grown woman in my thirties, I believe that God took me across that pool in slow motion to let me know, without a doubt, that it was He who held me in His arms when I needed Him.

Touched by the Lord

When I was about twelve years old, my family and I (my mother, Darlene, and my brother, Curtis) left our old church and began attending Mt. Carmel. The services were certainly different. At our previous church, my brother and I would sometimes lay our heads on our mother's lap when we grew tired. We had spent a lot of energy in Sunday school, and when it was time for the message, my attention was spent. Although there was much that I did not understand about spiritual things, I knew that God loved me. By the time I began attending Mt. Carmel, I had developed better listening skills. I was no longer tempted to lay my head on my mother's lap. I found myself focusing on the pastor's words. As I listened to him preach, I understood clearly God's plan of salvation.

Eventually, I surrendered my heart to the Lord, and I was saved at Mt. Carmel. On the day that I received salvation, the preacher had asked everyone in the church to line up so that he could lay hands on each of them, anoint them, and pray for them. We all were in line, and as I approached the front of the line, I heard one of the ministers say to me, "Raise your hands and say **yes** to the Lord." When I raised my hands to the Lord, I lost sight of everything and everybody. When I came to myself, I was standing in front of the church with my hands raised, tears streaming down my face. I realized the Lord had saved me. I remember looking at the people in the congregation who had already been prayed for, and my eyes fell on my cousin Tiffani, who was looking right at me. I smiled and went to my seat feeling good.

I believe God sent my family to this church for a reason. God knew that I would be able to comprehend what the pastor was saying, and God had a word for me to hear. There were times when the pastor preached that the Word would penetrate my spirit, and tears would just start streaming down my face. I thank the Lord for loving me enough to allow me to come to know Him and to develop a relationship with Him as a little girl.

The Birth of My Son

When I was nineteen years old I gave birth to my first child, a baby boy whom I named Jeffrey. During my pregnancy, I did not have any complications until I went into labor. I went into labor on July 20, 1990. It was nighttime, the weekend of our family reunion, and I was in bed when the labor pains began. I felt pressure in my stomach, so I went to the bathroom. When fluid erupted from my body, I thought the birthing process had begun, and my mother rushed me to the hospital.

After the doctor had examined me, he told me that I was not ready to deliver the baby. I had dilated only one centimeter. I was sent home—only to return the next day because of the pain I was experiencing. This time, the hospital decided to admit me. I was in severe pain, but the doctors did not want me to have the baby yet. I was in my eighth month, and the baby had not turned. The doctor prescribed some medication to prevent the contractions, but the medicine, administered intravenously (IV), did not control the terrible pain. Every few minutes I would have a really bad contraction. Almost every time I felt an intense pain, I would call out for my mother. After awhile she became a bit impatient with me and told me to quit calling her because there was nothing she could do. Terribly frustrated, I started fussing, because I wanted the nurses to do something about the pain. I endured the pain off and on throughout the night.

The next morning I was still in pain, but the doctors did not think I was ready to have the baby. My mother and my aunt were doing what they could to help comfort me. My mother was massaging my legs because I had leg cramps. My Aunt Sharon was massaging my mother's back as she bent over to massage me. Finally, after hours of intense pain, my body was ready to give birth.

I will never forget the feeling I experienced. My whole body felt strange. It was a feeling I had never felt before. It is hard to explain the feeling, but I knew the baby was ready to come forth, and I was ready to push. I had not received an epidural, but I needed to push. I kept telling the nurse the baby was coming, but she did not believe me. Then she checked me and felt the baby's feet. They started trying to prepare me for a Caesarean section because my baby was breeched, but it was too late. I had to give birth vaginally.

At 7:23 P.M. on July 22, 1990, my baby boy, weighing in at five pounds and ten ounces, entered the world. His birth truly had been a miracle. I had been only eight months along and my baby boy was born healthy. I thanked God that my baby was alive, well and healthy. I do not even want to think about what could have happened because the doctors were unprepared, thinking I was not ready to give birth. Even though they were wrong, God had His hand on my life and my unborn son's life. He protected us and allowed him to be born healthy. What the devil had meant for evil, God made it good.

About a year after Jeffrey was born, we traveled to Tulsa, Oklahoma, with his father to visit his family so that they could see the baby. On our way back home, the baby began crying and nothing we did would stop him from crying. Fearing that something was seriously wrong with him, we stopped at a hospital in a small town in Kansas. The doctor who treated him gave him a suppository and sent us on our way.

When we arrived in Kansas City, the baby was still experiencing complications, so I took him to his pediatrician. He examined the baby and advised us to go to the hospital immediately. The nurse called for an ambulance to transport my baby to Children's Mercy Hospital, where he would undergo emergency surgery on his intestines. My mother and I followed the ambulance. Before the medical attendants took my son into the operating room, they allowed me to see him. I took a good look at him, kissed him, and said, "Everything is going to be all right." When the hospital attendant wheeled my one-year-old son down the hall to the operating room, I could restrain myself no longer. I broke down and began to cry a flood of tears. My heart ached for my baby, but I knew he was in safe hands.

Throughout the ordeal, my family and I had prayed for little Jeffrey, believing that he would come out of this alive, and that he would be a healthy little boy. Praise God, He answered our prayers. Jeffrey came through surgery successfully. The doctor said if we had waited twenty-four hours more, my baby could have died. I thanked God for preserving his life and letting the doctors know what was wrong with him so they could correct the problem.

Thank You, Lord, for keeping my son and blessing him to live a long and prosperous life—in Jesus' name. Amen. Praise God!

How I Discovered My Ministry

By 1995 I had been saved for some time, but I did not know what my ministry to the body of Christ was. One day when I was at the beauty salon, I saw a man watching a videotape by Bishop T.D.Jakes. During a conversation with him, he gave me his mother's business card for her tape ministry. Ever since that time I have collected and watched Bishop Jakes' videos. His tapes have truly blessed me and brought me to a closer relationship with God. The Lord sent this ministry into my life to plant the Word down in my soul and spirit. I began sharing the videos with others, who also confessed to being blessed by the messages. When I began sharing the tapes, I was unaware at the time that this would be the beginning of my ministry.

Years later, I was sitting at home watching a T.D. Jakes tape on the night of our Women of Excellence (WOE) meeting, a monthly women's fellowship at our church. I had planned to stay at home that night, but at the last minute, something came over me and said, "Go to the women's meeting." I dressed quickly and went to the meeting that Thursday night. God had ordained that I attend the meeting that night.

Our first lady was speaking that night. Near the end of the services, she called forth people who wanted prayer for their ministries. There were three lines, depending upon the nature of the prayer request. People who could identify their ministries and were already operating in them were instructed to form a line. The second line was designated for people who knew what their ministry was, but they were not operating in it. The third line included those people who didn't know what their ministry was. The third line was for me. I didn't know what ministry God had for me, but I surely wanted to know what my ministry was.

When the first lady approached me to pray for me, she encouraged me by saying that I had a sincere heart, and that God had forgiven me of my sins. She proclaimed to every woman in the house that God had forgiven us of our sins, and that He had thrown them into the sea of forgetfulness. I do not recall everything she said to me, but what she said caused my heart to rejoice and helped to build my faith even higher.

About two weeks later, as I was watching a video by Bishop Jakes, the Lord whispered into my ear the words "tape ministry." I had heard His voice very distinctly, as He told me what my ministry was to be. I believed in my heart that God had spoken to me. After the Lord had told me what one of my ministries would be I called the lady with the tape ministry and told her what happened at church two weeks prior to hearing God's voice. She was so happy for me and said that the idea really must have come from the Lord because she had been considering discontinuing her tape ministry. She was sure that the Lord had sent me to continue this ministry.

The lady shared some of her experiences with me and helped me get started in the tape ministry. I believe that God granted me favor with this woman so that I could begin the ministry He had designed for me.

God Lifts Burdens

In the spring of 1996, when the company I was working for relocated to another state, I found myself looking for another job. I soon landed a job as a junior accounting clerk, and everything appeared to be going well. I had thought that this business would be a stable workplace for me. The people there seemed friendly at first, but as time went on, I soon found out that this was not the case.

None of the jobs I had held previously had been complicated. Everything had been laid-back, with no major changes that affected me. When I began my new job in 1996, I soon learned that deviating from a normal routine could be hard on the one hand and good on the other. At my previous job, I had grown accustomed to procedures, personnel and job responsibilities. When I started my new job, I was not accustomed to very much diversification; therefore, it was very difficult for me, in the beginning, to become acclimated to the changes that were to come.

While I was a junior accounting clerk, my department experienced three different supervisors, and, of course, each one had a different view on how the department should be run. The shifts in department leadership affected the morale of the workers. Co-workers were changing departments and/or leaving the company. Eventually, I was promoted to the position of senior accounting clerk, which came with a big raise in pay (this change was good). Of course, the devil was not pleased because of the happiness my promotion and resulting increase in pay. He began to attack me in my emotions. The pressure of adjusting to a different job began to take its toll on me, stressing me to the point that I did not want to return to work.

The burden of change on my job bore heavy on my shoulders. One evening I went home to my apartment, lay on my bed and started praying to God to lift this burden, and help me deal with the situation in which I found myself. Shortly after I had finished praying, my phone rang, and it was my mother on the other end. I explained all that had been going on at my job and how it was affecting me. Immediately, my mother led me to Isaiah 41:10-13 (NIV), and we hung up the phone so that I could read the verses of Scripture.

> *So do not fear, for I am with you; do not be dismayed, for I am your God. I will strengthen you and help you; I will uphold you with my righteous right hand. All who rage against you will surely be ashamed and disgraced; those who oppose you will be as nothing and perish. Though you search for your enemies, you will not find them. Those who wage war against you will be as nothing at all. For I am the LORD, your God, who takes hold of your right hand and says to you, Do not fear; I will help you.*

I began to praise God as tears of joy streamed down my face. I loved God so much, and I knew that He loved me so much that He sent a special scripture just for me—to comfort me in a time when I needed Him most.

I did not realize how stressed I had become until I read the Scriptures. Immediately, the burden was lifted off me, and my body began to shift into a relaxation mode. I felt one hundred percent better; I literally felt the load lift off my shoulders. I knew without a doubt that the Lord answered my prayer by giving that scripture to my mother to give to me. God is so good and awesome that even with something as little as my job bothering me, He sent His Word to comfort me. He relieved me of the stress that had burdened me, and I thanked Him with all my heart, soul, and body.

Sometimes we think that situations are so terrible that we cannot take them to anyone, but to God they are nothing. God let me know that nothing is impossible for Him to handle. He let me know that the battle was not mine, but His, and all I had to do was cast all my cares on Him and He would take care of everything. Praise God!

Laid Off

After nearly three years as a senior accountant clerk, around the end of 1999, I received notice that I was being laid off my job. At that time, I was a single mother with a child (Jeffrey) to support. Fortunately for me, I had moved back home shortly before I was laid off so that I could begin to save money to buy a house.

At first, I had thought that my moving back home would reflect badly on me because I was grown, and I had a child. I was worried about what people would think about me. Sometimes things happen in your life unexpectedly and force you to do things you really do not want to do. But in my case, moving back home was a blessing in disguise. My parents agreed to let me live with them rent-free until I could get back on my feet.

As I look back, I realize how much of a blessing moving back home really was. I had moved before I was laid off my job. Although I did not have to pay rent, I still had other bills to pay, and I had to provide for my son. I desperately needed my own income, so I went job hunting. I had several interviews but no job offers. During the interim, I decided to file for unemployment.

With lots of free time on our hands, and a steady but temporary income, my mother and I were free to engage in an activity which we had often looked forward to doing—going shopping whenever we wanted. I had once dated a guy whose mother and sister did not have to work, and it seemed that they would go shopping almost every week. My mother and I would always say we wish we could live that type of life. Well, our wish had been granted. While I was waiting for a job offer and receiving unemployment checks, my mother and I would go shopping almost every week. We were sensible in our spending because we knew that we had financial responsibilities. As we shopped, we would think back and say, "Remember when we used to wish we could go shopping and not have to work? Just look at us now!" Then we would look at each other and burst into laughter. My mother and I were able to bond in a way that we had not done before. I considered the time I spent with my mother a blessing from God. He had given my mother and me a time to enjoy each other without a care in the world. We enjoyed that time while it lasted. I continued to receive unemployment checks, and during that time, I tithed faithfully.

About five weeks after I had been receiving the checks, I received a letter from the employment office stating that my case had to be predetermined to check whether or not I had really qualified for the first five weeks. The clerk informed me that if it were determined that I did not qualify to receive payment, I would have to pay back all the money I had received. Five weeks went by without my receiving any more checks. I prayed in faith, asking the Lord to give me favor. At the end of the five weeks, the employment office sent me a letter stating I would have a telephone interview with the employment agency and a company I had worked for in the past. I didn't know what the future held for me, but I trusted in a God who held the future in His hands.

There was a feeling of expectancy as I prepared for our weekly family prayer meeting. I knew that I would join my faith with the faith of my prayer partners and God would move in my behalf. I requested that they agree with me in prayer after I had made known my petitions. We agreed in prayer that the following would happen: (1) I would not have to pay back any of the money I had received for the first five weeks; (2) the employment office would pay me retroactively for the five weeks I had not received pay; and (3) the phone interview would be in my favor.

During the interview, we determined there was a misunderstanding about the dates of employment for the company that had laid me off. When the company confirmed my period of employment, the information on my record was corrected, and the case was closed. I was not required to pay any money back, and I received back pay for the five weeks I had to wait while the employment office sought to determine if I were qualified. God had answered my prayers. I believed that God would answer my prayers during that five-week period, and He did. He gave me favor with the employment office. I received one lump sum for the five weeks I had been denied payment. Praise God!

My Dream Business

I have always dreamed of owning a business—not just any business, but a salon and spa housed in a spacious, new building in an area accessible to many neighborhoods. My salon and spa would be a place where people could come and pamper themselves from head to toe. Whether my clientele wanted to try out one of the latest hairstyles, or just wanted to bask in a sauna or whirlpool, they would have the opportunity to do so at my salon and spa. I would offer a range of services, including manicures, pedicures, facials, and massages. Every woman would make it her business to visit my business because there would be no other place in town like it. The name on the marquee would read "Shontelle's Salon & Spa."

People would be drawn to my salon and spa, not only because of its services but also because of its environment. Christian music playing throughout the building would create an atmosphere of peace and serenity. I can visualize an area where people could watch Christian tapes, for example, tapes by T.D. Jakes and other recording artists. There would be plenty of wholesome reading material available. Of course, there would be a snack bar with a variety of snacks, including healthy ones. Although my business would be open to all ethnic groups, my specialty would be taking care of the hair and skin of Black people. I would love to have a beautiful place where Blacks could have their hair styled by someone who knows what to do with it. While they're having their hair done, they could get a pedicure, manicure, massage, or relax in a whirlpool or sauna. This is my dream business that I believe the Lord is going to bless me to have. In fact, I am speaking this business into existence now in Jesus' Name. I have already begun preparing myself for the time when God will bring this dream to pass.

My interest in fingernails reaches back to my childhood. When I was a little girl, I used to make fake nails out of Elmer's glue. I would squeeze the glue out onto the outside of a shoebox top and let the glue dry. When I thought the glue had dried sufficiently, I would cut off a piece of the dried glue, shape it to fit my nail, and then try to glue it onto my nail. That procedure never worked because the glue was too soft and my fake nail would always bend. Later, I would sometimes ask my mother if I could wear fake nails, and she would buy them for me. I was a little tomboy sometimes, however, (I say sometimes because I loved to play with Barbie dolls, too), and when I would go outside and play with my brother and our friends, my fake nails would eventually break off.

As I grew older, I dreamed of becoming a nail technician. I practiced on my nails. This time, however, I had switched from using 'Elmer's glue nails' to commercial nails. Actually, I became very good at doing my own nails—so good that everyone who saw my French tips thought they had been professionally done. When I was a senior in high school, I wrote a book report on nails. Throughout my early life working on nails has been a passion of mine. Naturally, when I became an adult, I wanted to incorporate my passion and know-how into my own business.

By the time I finished high school, I knew I would be going to school to become a nail technician. I knew I would need to work fulltime in order to pay for my tuition; however, I did not want to attend school and work at the same time because that would have taken too much time away from my son. To become a nail technician required 390 hours of education and training, and to qualify for financial help, you needed to have 500 or more hours. I knew I had to pay tuition, but I also knew that nothing is impossible with my God.

I went to our regular weekly prayer meeting. This week my prayer request was for me to be able to go to school fulltime without having to work, and have enough money to pay my other bills after the tuition had been paid. I knew that was a lot to ask, but I had a big dream and I knew that I served a *big* God. God understood my heart, He knew my dream, and He wants to see it come to fruition. I had faith in God and believed that nothing was impossible for Him. God's Word says, in Mark 11:24 (NIV), ". . . . .whatever you ask for in prayer, believe that you have received it, and it will be yours." That night at prayer, there were only three of us: Mashan, Tammy and I. We touched and agreed in prayer that God would bless me and give me favor by granting my prayer request.

God blessed me, indeed, and granted my request. I know I am not worthy of His blessings, but God loves me so much that He blessed me to attend school full-time without having to work, and He saw to it that my bills and tuition were paid. I praise God for giving me favor and loving me so much that He answers my prayers. I know that if God answers my prayers, He will surely answer your prayers. Because God answered my prayer, I now have my manicurist license. God proved faithful to His Word. As I continue to prepare myself in pursuit of my dream of becoming the owner of Shontelle's Salon & Spa, I know that God will be with me. He has never failed me yet. Praise God!

A Forgiving God

Shortly after we had been praying for about two years, I fell prey to the strategies Satan was wielding against us to destroy our prayer group. I backslid and had a baby out of wedlock. Even in the midst of my sins, I felt the Lord's hand drawing me back to Him. I loved the Lord with all my heart, and the desire of my heart had always been to do His will; therefore, I was miserable because I knew I was outside the will of God. I knew that what I was doing was wrong, and I did not want to be in that position.

I continued to pray, meaning every word, and believing that God was going to bring me out of this situation. The burden I carried was heavy, one I knew that I did not have to bear alone, for God's Word says in Matthew 11:28-30:

> *Come unto me, all ye that labour and are heavy laden, and I will give you rest. Take my yoke upon you, and learn of me; for I am meek and lowly in heart: and ye shall find rest unto your souls. For my yoke is easy, and my burden is light.*

If I surrendered my burden to the Lord, I knew He would carry it for me. Even when I was doing wrong, I was well aware of my actions, but my heart was not in what I was doing. My heart was with God. I know that this may sound contradictory, but I did not want to backslide; it was just something that happened. I had allowed the devil to detour me. His aim was to keep me from the destiny God has planned for my life.

Our prayer group knew from the outset that we would be in warfare against the devil, and what happened to me was one of his tactics to try to tear the prayer group apart. The Lord had given me a vision early on that Satan would attack us individually and that was the reason God said that we should pray for one another. In the vision, the Lord warned us that the devil would come against us with different strategies, and we could not afford to let our guard down. I know that the devil is a liar and a defeated foe. I survived his attack. I didn't give in; I didn't give up hope.

I am not bitter about what the devil tried to do in my life. I know he is angry because his tactic didn't work, but I also know that he won't give up; he'll try something else. With God on our side, we have the victory. God's word says in James 4:7-12:

> *Submit yourselves therefore to God. Resist the devil, and he will flee from you. Draw nigh to God, and he will draw nigh to you. Cleanse your hands, ye sinners; and purify your hearts, ye double minded. Be afflicted, and mourn, and weep: let your laughter be turned to mourning, and your joy to heaviness. Humble yourselves in the sight of the Lord, and he shall lift you up. Speak not evil one of another, brethren. He that speaketh evil of his brother, and judgeth his brother, speaketh evil of the law, and judgeth the law: but if thou judge the law, thou art not a doer of the law, but a judge.*

I asked God to forgive me for my sins, to cleanse me, and wash me with His blood. I followed the Word according to Acts 3, verse 19: "Repent ye therefore, and be converted, that your sins may be blotted out, when the times of refreshing shall come from the presence of the Lord."

I believe in my heart that God has forgiven me for my sins. What the devil meant for evil, God turned it into good. Romans 8:28 says, "And we know that all things work together for good to those who love God, to those who are the called according to His purpose." I know that I have been called to purpose in the kingdom of God.

When my beautiful baby girl was born March 10, 2002, I became the mother of two wonderful children, a pre-teen son and an infant daughter. (My son is now twelve years old, and my daughter, seven months.) They truly are a gift from God. I have returned to the Lord; and I am saved and living my life for Jesus. Although I walked away from Him, I know in my heart that the Lord never left me. He has always been in my heart and He always will be. God knows my heart and knows that I want to do His will and live my life for Him.

I truly thank the Lord for being a merciful and **forgiving God**. He is so wonderful. He still loves me, in spite of my wrongdoing. I thank Him because He is the God of second chances. I thank God for forgiving me of my sins, and for covering me with His blood. God's Word says in Psalms 85:2, "Thou hast forgiven the iniquity of thy people; thou hast covered all their sin. Selah." Thank You, Lord that my sins are covered by the blood of Jesus. Thank you for your love and mercy.

My Townhouse

Although eight months had passed since the horrible incident of September 11, 2001, the economy was yet suffering fallout. I knew that finding another good-paying job with excellent benefits, one similar to the job I had held before, would be difficult. Thus, I found myself seeking employment through a temporary agency (temp) to support my two children and myself. I began working through a temporary service at the end of May in 2002. Although the job I took was scheduled to end in two months, there was a slight chance it could last longer or even become permanent. Deep in my heart, I hoped that the job would turn into a permanent one for me.

When my second child was born, I had been living with my parents for about two years. Now that there were three of us—my son, my daughter, and I—we needed more space. Many things had been going on in my life, different trials and tribulations, and I felt the need to be on my own.

My relationship with my parents has always been good. Generally speaking, we get along with one another very well because I respect them as parents; however, living with your parents when you're an adult with two children can sometimes be difficult.

There certainly were times when we had our disagreements, usually over small things. For example, after you reach a certain age, you want to live by your own rules—not someone else's rules. Something in you rebels when someone else tells you what to do. Likewise, you do not want anyone else telling you how to raise your children. Deep down in my heart, I really knew that the advice my mother had always given me was best for us, but I wanted the opportunity to make my own decisions about what was best for my children and me.

I had my own space upstairs in my parents' house. It was almost like a small apartment. There were two large rooms and a huge closet, but no bathroom or kitchen. (I think God knew my parents would need that big house. They have had so many family members live with them throughout the thirty some years they have been there.) Nevertheless, I was a grown woman now with two children and I knew I needed to have my own place.

I imagined that several years would pass before I would be able to move out of my parents' home and live on my own. Driving back and forth to work, I would pass by a construction site where new townhouses were being built. One day as I passed by, I saw the now-leasing sign. In the past, my mother and I had always enjoyed touring beautiful, new homes, believing that the Lord would bless us to live in one some day. When the new townhouses were finished, maybe they would be next on our list to tour.

After several weeks had gone by, my curiosity got the best of me. I wanted to see the inside of the townhouses. I knew that I probably would not be financially approved because I was working a temporary job, but I decided to take a look at one anyway. My mother, son, and daughter went with me. We all liked what we had seen, and before I knew it, I was asking for an application to move in.

The clerk explained the paperwork to me and advised me of all the supporting documents I needed to bring with me when I returned with my application. Keep in mind I had been on my temporary job for just a month at this point. The manager at the townhouses said that the application process would take about sixty days. In a few days I returned to the leasing office with everything the clerk had requested and left without worrying whether or not I would be approved.

When I began receiving calls from the leasing office asking me to clarify certain parts of my application, my hopes soared. The excitement grew as I waited, and I wanted more and more to move into one of the townhouses.   Periodically, the thought of my application being rejected would come to discourage me momentarily: "But you work for a temporary service, and you know they are not going to approve your application." I would shake the thought and continue my pursuit. I kept in contact with the manager to check on the progress of my application. I began to pray and ask God to allow me to move there. I prayed for favor with the managers so that I could get approved for a three-bedroom townhouse.

Almost two months had gone by when I received the call that I had been waiting for. One of the managers of the townhouse was calling me to let me know that my application had been approved. What I thought would have taken years to happen, took only a few months— because God was in the plan.

Because God had helped me make the first step, I believed that He would make a way for me to make the rental payments until He moved me to some place better. I rejoiced in my new home, knowing that, according to James, chapter one, verse 17, my new home was a gift from God: "Every good gift and every perfect gift is from above, and cometh down from the Father of lights, with whom is no variableness, neither shadow of turning." He had given me a brand new place for me to live with my children. I began thanking and praising God for giving me favor with the managers, and for those who granted my approval to live there. What a good and awesome God we serve!

After receiving the key to my new home, my mother and I went inside, praying and blessing every room as we walked from room to room. I said to my mother, "Wow, this is really mine to live in! I'm not wishing it were mine; it really is *mine*." This was the first new place I had ever lived in, and God had blessed little *ole* me to stay there. Thank You, Jesus. This was another one of God's miracles that He had wrought in my life. I had been approved even though I had two children, was working for a temporary agency, and had been doing so for only a few months. Moreover, God gave me favor, even when in the natural, the situation seemed impossible, for with God nothing is impossible. I give Him all the praise!

Loosed in Jesus' Name

Our weekly prayer meeting was to be held at my house that fall night in 2002. It was the twenty-fourth of October and the weather was cold, dark and rainy. Although the weather outside was dreary, inside my house was warm, cozy and inviting. In spite of the weather, the other five prayer partners arrived at my house safely. We were into our third year praying. It seemed that the time had passed so quickly that I could hardly believe that it had been three years since the

Lord had given me the vision for us to come together to pray for one another.

I had spent the entire week in great anticipation. I knew that I was scheduled to pray that night, and I wanted to be prepared and ready to pray. I remembered my Sunday school teacher telling me when I was a little girl to ask God to teach me how to pray. Before that time, I had never really thought about asking God to teach me how to pray. I will always remember my Sunday school teacher for teaching me this about prayer. That week, I put her advice into practice. I had been asking God to teach me how to pray because I wanted to *sound* good as I expressed my true feeling to God from my heart. I also wanted to pray for the needs and desires of the group.

Sometimes on my job during breaks, I would listen to Christian messages on the Internet. This particular week on Thursday, I scrolled through religious messages on the Internet and found one entitled, "Teach Me How to Pray". I knew the Lord had sent this message my way so that I could get a better understanding about prayer. As I listened to the message, I learned that God does not care how you *sound* when you pray, or even if your words are spoken well. What God does care about is whether or not the prayer is coming from your heart, because God already knows what we need and what we want. Listening to this message, and others similar to it, and praising God in my heart, I felt God delivering me from obstacles in my life. I felt such a relief in my spirit, and I knew that the Holy Spirit had come to comfort me through the Word of God recorded in II Corinthians 1:3 and 4 (NKJV):

Blessed be the God and Father of our Lord Jesus Christ, the Father of mercies and God of all comfort, who comforts us in all our tribulation, that we may be able to comfort those who are in any trouble, with the comfort with which we ourselves are comforted by God.

That night the six of us had gathered for prayer, not knowing exactly how the Holy Spirit would lead us, but we were open to whatever He wanted to do in us and through us. Before we prayed, we watched a powerful message by Bishop T.D. Jakes, entitled "Favor Ain't Fair," tape number three from the series, *Nothing Just Happens.* After we had finished viewing the tape, we worshipped and praised God.

When I began to pray, I started out with the Lord's Prayer. Then I paused and began praying for God to cleanse us on the inside and take out what was not like Him and fill us with the fruit of the Spirit. After I had prayed awhile, other members of the prayer group began to pray. Then the Holy Spirit prompted me to pray the following short prayer: "Lord, if anyone of us is harboring any unforgiveness, Lord, please help us to forgive because Your Word says that if we don't forgive others, You won't forgive us. In Jesus Name I pray, thank God. Amen." As we sat there praying, my cousin Tiffani began praying in tongues, allowing the Holy Spirit to intercede for us in areas where we needed His help.

In the past when I had a problem forgiving others, I went through the Bible and read every verse of Scripture on *forgiveness.* After that experience, I set in my mind to forgive and not hold any grudges against

anyone. Two verses of Scripture that always remained
with me were found in the Gospel of Mark:

> *And whenever you stand praying, if you*
> *have anything against anyone, forgive him that*
> *your Father in heaven may also forgive you your*
> *trespasses. But if you do not forgive, neither will*
> *your Father in heaven forgive your trespasses*
> (Mark 11:25, 26, NKJV).

I knew that I wanted the Lord to forgive me of all my
sins; therefore, I had to forgive others for the negative
things they had done or said to me.

That night during prayer, we implemented a new
procedure. The members of the group would encircle the
host, holding hands, and pray a special prayer for her.
We would touch and agree in prayer for many things—
God's favor, God's choice blessings, a greater anointing,
and fulfillment of purpose in her life.

After Tiffani had finished praying in tongues, the
group put me in the middle of the circle so they could
pray for me. My mother began the prayer, my Aunt
Sharon followed. After they had finished praying, the
Lord gave Tiffani a revelation. She said, "God wants us
to motion our hands to pull down the strongholds off
Shontelle". They began pulling down strongholds in the
natural while God was pulling them down in the Spirit,
so that I could become the woman God had called me to
be. The stronghold for me was fear. God delivered me
and set me free, in Jesus' Name. I could declare these
words: "For God has not given us a spirit of fear, but of
power and of love and of a sound mind" (II Tim. 1:7,
NKJV).

Touching and Agreeing

The prayer group decided to have prayer on Christmas Eve instead of our regular prayer night so that we could exchange gifts. This time it was Aunt Sharon's turn to host prayer. As we sat around the kitchen talking, Tiffani said the Lord had told her to touch and agree with me in prayer for a permanent position with the company I had been working for through a temporary agency. I agreed, and nothing else was said about the prayer agreement that day.

I went to work Thursday of the same week, e-mailed Tiffani, and asked her if she remembered what God had said to her about touching and agreeing with me to be hired permanently with the company where I was already working. I had agreed with Tiffani. But what she did not know was that I also had been praying for a permanent job with the same company. I needed the stability and the benefits which this job had to offer. In addition, God had blessed me to live in a new townhouse, and I needed permanent income.

Friday of that week, Tiffani responded to my e-mail, saying, "Yes, that is what I said. I believe the Lord is going to bless you with a full-time position before the year is out. Let's believe God together."

That following Monday, two supervisors approached me and took me to a conference room to talk to me privately. They asked if I wanted to work on a different assignment, one that could possibly be permanent. I said, "Yes!" God had answered our prayers.

God's giving me the permanent job was just one example of how good God is. When you obey Him and do what He says, He will surely answer your prayers. This situation also proves how powerful it is to have prayer partners with whom you can touch and agree to petition God for needs in your life. I thank God for my prayer group. The Lord called us together for a reason and, repeatedly, He has 'blown our minds' with His wonderful blessings through answered prayers.

A Special Prayer Answered

When we began our prayer group, we prayed many prayers, and one of those personal prayers included praying for husbands for those of us who were single. Of the six of us, three (including myself) were single and I wanted a husband. We all prayed, believing that our prayers would be answered. We did not know when we would get married or who our husbands would be. We had faith that the Lord would bless us with saved, loving, godly, husbands.

Over a period of time, God had blessed us so much, repeatedly giving us favor and miracles, that my faith had grown over the years of praying with my family. My relationship with God had become closer. I fell in love with Him over and over again because He is a wonderful, loving, and forgiving God.

When we began our prayer group, I was dating a young man, not knowing whether or not he was 'the right one.' I had been dating him for about three years, hoping he was the one for me to marry. We had talked about marriage several times during our relationship, but he never popped the question. At the time, I was thirty-one years old and had two children, one who is his (my youngest who is now 10 months old). After three years, I had begun to wonder, "Lord, is he really the one? Are You going to bless us to get married and raise our daughter together in a happy marriage?" I knew I was getting older and I still wanted to have more children—at least one more. God had blessed us so much already, and I felt that if we kept the faith, He would answer this prayer, and we would be married some day.

One night at the beginning of January, prayer was at my house. That night I decided to pray a special prayer. While I was praying aloud, I asked the other women in the group to touch and agree with me in prayer concerning my relationship with my friend. My request was for us to get married immediately, and as a couple, be saved and sanctified, living our lives for the Lord and raising our children to know the Lord, in Jesus' Name.

When my friend showed up at my house January 14, 2003, with a small box with an engagement ring inside, I must admit that I was surprised. He asked me to marry him. All I could do was scream, "Yes! Yes! Yes!" God had answered my special prayer.

Later that day I began to thank and praise the Lord for answering my prayers. I praised Him for being so good to me, for being so faithful and just to forgive me of my sins. I knew that I did not deserve all of His goodness, but He had blessed me anyway. He had given me favor and had worked miracles in my life that had brought me to my knees praising and worshipping Him. My fiancé and I were married March 29, 2003.

I thank You, Lord, for all that You have done for my family and me.

Conclusion

Family Circle of Prayer

I love you, Sister...I love you, Cousin....
I love you, Auntie...I love you, Niece...
I love you, Daughter...

Conclusion

We Praise God for Bringing Us Together

We marvel at the fact that God chose us to stand in the gap and pray for our family. We were not strangers to prayer, for we had heard and seen its power in action all our lives. But it seems that the real essence of the power of prayer and what it could accomplish in the lives of God's people had somehow eluded us as we had taken prayer too lightly. We had not considered this powerful tool at our hands, nor had we thought of how this power could be multiplied when six women stood together in prayer. The importance of prayer had not sunk deeply into our spirits until God brought us into that revealing knowledge. Today, we glorify Him for reminding us of our God-given authority over Satan, which Christ accomplished for us at Calvary, and for giving us the resources to stop Satan in his tracks.

How many fiery darts from the enemy have been thwarted? We don't know. From how many unseen dangers have we been protected? We don't know, but we do know that He is our shield and sword, and we praise Him for opening our eyes to the need for family prayer, and for showing us the power of women coming together in prayer. Although our prayers of salvation for our family have not all come to fruition, we are all still praying and believing that the job is done. God's longsuffering toward us has blessed us to this point, and we are in it for the long haul. Our family and friends are just that important to us. We will not give up, for our eternal hope is in Christ Jesus, and in Him, we know we are victorious. All of the glory and the honor belong to

God, and we thank and praise Him for His blessings.

Our family has been blessed beyond measure, yet God just keeps on blessing us. If you are facing circumstances which weigh heavily on your heart, be encouraged. What God has done for us, He will do for you because He stands by His Word to perform it—"...The effectual fervent prayers of a righteous man [or woman] availeth much" (James 5:16b).

Sharon Gooch